A Special Gift

For

_____

From

_____

Date

_____

Cheerful Hearts

Copyright © 1967, 1993 by Leroy Brownlow
Formerly titled *Better Than Medicine — A Merry Heart*

Quality Publications
1-800-359-7708
P.O. Box 7385 · Fort Worth, TX 76111

Printed in the United States of America.
ISBN 0-915720-07-8

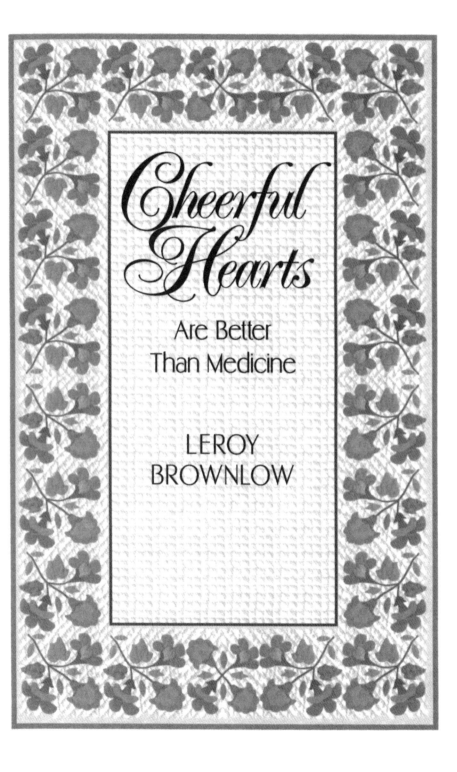

Cheerful Hearts

Are Better
Than Medicine

LEROY
BROWNLOW

Gift Books

A Psalm in My Heart
Flowers for Mother
Flowers for You
Flowers of Friendship
Flowers That Never Fade
For Mom With Love
Give Us This Day
Grandpa Was a Preacher
Jesus Wept
Leaves of Gold
Making the Most of Life
Thoughts of Gold—Wisdom for Living
Today and Forever
Today Is Mine
University of Hard Knocks

Contents

Foreword

*C*heerful *Hearts* is a volume devoted to the value of happiness and to the principles in attaining it. Centuries ago Solomon said:

> *A merry heart does good like medicine,*
> *but a broken spirit dries the bones.*
> —PROVERBS 17:22

Joy is the best therapy. A spoonful of happiness is better than a spoonful of drugs; but it does not come that easily in such ready forms — liquid, pill or capsule.

Medicines are of great benefit to us in treating our ailments; but when the underlying cause is emotional turmoil, then drugs can only relieve the symptoms — not cure the cause. In such a case, the person's basic need is peace.

The Romans bequeathed to us an enlightening thought in the living proverb: "A sound mind in a sound body." It is a recognized fact that the health of mind and body are inseparable.

About the middle of the nineteenth century, Claude Bernard, a French physician, began to speak of the mind's part in ailments which manifested themselves in the body. He has been acclaimed as one of the first in his profession to understand something of this fact and to make use of the information in treatment.

Books grow. This one is the outgrowth of thirty years of

spiritual and psychological counseling in which I was brought face to face with large numbers of people in a great metropolitan area who were confronted with problems of every sort. The advice given has been tried and tested in the most practical laboratory in the world, human lives with all their ups and downs, and has been found satisfactory and helpful to hundreds of people. For illustrative instances, I have mostly drawn from my own observation and counseling, but have taken every care to guard anonymity.

I have the deep conviction that every one of us can attain happiness, peace and tranquility. Each is in his own little world, good or bad, because of what he is, and the only way he can move from a world of frustration to a world of peace is to change himself. Inasmuch as cheerfulness is a personal quality, then each must look for it within himself — if he would find it.

The first chapter is devoted to the recognized relationship of emotions to bodily health and the rest of the book for the achievement of the inwardly coherent and peaceful personality, free of internal harassment and distraction.

Wherever possible, I have chosen to use the simplest language instead of technical terms that this material may be as readable, practical and enjoyable as possible.

LEROY BROWNLOW

ONE   *Better Than Medicine*

    A merry heart does good like a medicine, but a broken spirit dries the bones" (Proverbs 17:22). This is Solomon's ancient Biblical testimony to the dual treatment of human ills — a merry heart and medicine. The combined psychological and physiological views equal the psychosomatic approach to man's well-being.

• *"A merry heart doeth good like a medicine"* — this bears witness to the mental factor in health. A true philosophy of life is of great benefit to our physical and spiritual well-being. One of the decisive conditions of bodily health is a strong, integrated personality stemming from a happy and hardy and handsome mind.

A cheerful heart is a good preventive and a good corrective treatment — better than medicine. A contented and pleasant disposition protects one against disease, for the mind has a powerful influence over the body. If there are non-physical factors which cause disease, then there must be non-physical factors to cure it.

The merry heart is the life of a man and the prolongation of his days. Inasmuch as the whole person is involved in the prevention and cure of illness, then the emotions are included, too — and more and more this is being appreciated.

The Bible, in commenting on joy, the emotion so essential to our good interest, further says:

CHEERFUL HEARTS
♥♥♥♥♥♥♥♥♥♥♥♥♥♥♥♥♥♥♥♥♥♥♥♥♥

*A merry heart makes a cheerful countenance,
but by sorrow of the heart the spirit is broken.*
— PROVERBS 15:13

He who is of a merry heart has a continual feast.
— PROVERBS 15:15

*Why are you cast down, O my soul? and why
are you disquieted within me? Hope in God;
for I shall yet praise Him, the help of my
countenance, and my God.*
— PSALM 43:5

*They shall obtain joy and gladness, and sorrow
and sighing shall flee away.*
— ISAIAH 35:10

The Creator wants us to be happy. He started us in life
with a certain supply of health, energy, raw brain and raw
materials, which He wants us to use to our joy. One of His most
positive and repeated commands in the Bible is, "Rejoice."

• *"Like a medicine"* — this testifies to the medical
approach in treating our ills. Although the Bible, a textbook on
right living, chiefly concerns itself with the mind and soul of
man, it does recognize the value of medicine in spite of its
primitive state in that day. Luke was a physician (Colossians
4:14). In the story of *Who's My Neighbor* we learn that the
Good Samaritan treated the robbed and injured man by pour-
ing in oil and wine (Luke 10:34). The wine was an antiseptic
and the oil was a curative. The apostle Paul issued this command: "Use a little wine for your stomach's sake and your frequent infirmities" (I Timothy 5:23). This injunction, as we see,
was based on a medicinal need.

• *Psychic influences have a decided power in producing illness.* The tune in one's heart helps to determine the tone of one's health. Many of the bodily ills are emotionally caused.

Everyday observation has taught us that the body is affected by the mind. All of us have seen a fatigued physique caused by a broken spirit, physical nausea produced by worry, and the loss of appetite rooted in sorrow.

Outstanding physicians estimate that the ailments of three-fourths of the people in convalescence and one-half of them in acute illness originated in the mind rather than in the body.

Modern science has proved in the laboratory that mental moods have power to produce disease and poor health.

Experiments at major universities show that what goes on in the brain has a bearing on what goes on in the arteries. Scientific tests point to the complex role of the nervous system in accelerating arteriosclerosis and the triggering of heart attacks. In one experiment in which two groups of rabbits were fed exactly the same low-fat diets, the scientists stimulated with electrodes a certain part of the brain of one group. This gave off tiny electrical discharges which stimulated nerve impulses. The results were very revealing — in three months the stimulated group's cholesterol had risen three times as much as the other group, and the fat deposits in the arteries had accumulated four times as much.

The general conclusion is that the anxious, easily-excitable, over-competitive person is more prone to heart attack than the calm person.

Much of our fatigue is due to psychological reasons. Physicians report that the most common complaint they hear from their patients is, "I'm so tired." A chronic fatigue afflicts millions of people where there is no evidence of either physical malfunction or insufficient rest. Many tired people are just tired of their way of life — they need a cheerful contented disposition, something better than medicine.

Halitosis may be produced by many physical factors: dehydration, sinuses, teeth, lungs, stomach and intestines. But when nothing physically wrong can be found, halitosis may be due to strong emotions. Bitter hate, fiery anger and undisciplined worry produce an unpleasant breath.

Personality disorders may be caused by a guilty conscience. The one who decides to cheat on society suffers the fear of being caught— it disrupts the serene life and destroys health. A clear conscience is of great medical benefit in guarding the mind against neuroticism.

The list of diseases related to the emotions is a long one to which we can add *asthma, hay fever, sinus, headache, peptic ulcer, ulcerative colitis, constipation, diarrhea, hiccoughs, rheumatoid arthritis, backache, angina pectoris, hypertension, hives, eczema, cerebral strokes of apoplexy, hyperthyroidism, glaucoma* and many others. Of course, we should not assume that the emotional factor is the only cause in the development of any of these diseases.

Nervousness is not so apt to come from the nerves as the thoughts in the mind which affect the nerves.

Some time ago I was the guest for lunch in the home of a friend, a doctor of medicine. As we were eating, he stated that he had seen thirty-two patients that morning and that only one of them was really sick. Of course, what he meant was that only one was organically sick. "A cheerful heart" would go a long way in curing the most of them, for presently they have no organic problems; but shortly, unless those patients are made anew in their minds, functional disorders will develop.

• *Being endowed by the Creator to live life realistically, we were also given the fatiguing emotions of fear, anger, anxiety and sorrow.* The fact that we were supplied with these qualities is positive proof that there is a time for them to be used. The Bible says:

> *To every thing there is a season, and a time to every purpose under the heaven...a time to weep, and a time to laugh...a time to love, and a time to hate; a time of war, and a time of peace.*
> — ECCLESIASTES 3:1-8

Inasmuch as anger and fear were designed for our good, then we should not pervert them to our destruction. They were intended to be only emergency powers to exert the whole body for its protection. Increased blood circulation and added glucose, produced by rage or fear, strengthen the muscles to be used in struggle or flight; and the peripheral ischemia and the decrease in the blood clotting time lessens the consequences of the wounds that may be produced in combat. It is obvious, therefore, that nature has supplied us with emotional reactions to fill a needed function.

But they are not always needed. In everyday living these emotional responses of stress and strain to exaggerated danger signals are to no avail. There is the build up again and again of this temporary strength to no use, for there is no flight or struggle — just the dissipation of nervous energies to the gradual weakening of the ordinary strength one possesses. So what nature intended to be a blessing is misused and made a detriment.

High-strung emotions may appear when there is no external

cause to justify them, when there is only an internal conflict in which man battles himself; in such cases, peace of mind would have great therapeutic power — more than medicine.

• *Though there are exceptional circumstances which call for exceptional emotions, God's gift to us for general living is joy* as stated by Solomon:

> *And also that every man should eat and drink, and enjoy the good of all his labor, it is the gift of God.*
> — ECCLESIASTES 3:13

We have read that Dr. Marshall Hall many years ago frequently prescribed cheerfulness for his patients, saying that it was better than anything he could get at the drugstore. "Mirth is God's medicine," says a wise writer, "and everybody ought to bathe in it." It was a favorite saying of Bancroft, the historian, who was a vigorous old man at ninety, that the secret of a long life is found in cheerfulness and in never losing your temper.

More recently, Norman Cousins has demonstrated this fact again for a new generation. Sent home to die of an incurable illness, Cousins confounded his physicians by living and refusing to die. His prescription—a daily diet of laughter and activities that brought joy to his soul.

It would be a dark hour if we should decide that we cannot achieve a reasonable degree of happiness. Life would become a mere plodding toward the grave in which there is little more than the lifting of one foot in front of the other.

Music gives a kind of romance to an army on the march. It neither shortens the road nor throws out the rocks, but it saves the soldiers from tiring so quickly. The sound of music has a tendency to make them less mindful of the trying ordeals.

So it is with joy; it is music in the heart which makes man

less heedful of the stress of the journey.

The cheerful disposition protects health, prolongs life, adds warmth and vibrance to personality, increases success, stimulates life and multiplies our pleasantries. It does too much for us not to achieve it, and especially when it is within the attainment of every person.

Thus we propose in the remaining chapters to help every person find that which is better than medicine — a cheerful heart.

References
1. McMillens, S. I.: *None of These Diseases*, Fleming H. Revell Co., 1963.
2. Miles, Henry H. W.; Cobb, Stanley; Shands, Harley C., eds.: *Case Histories in Psychosomatic Medicine*, W. W. Norton & Co., 1952.
3. Cobb, S.: *Emotions and Clinical Medicine*, W. W. Norton & Co., 1950.
4. Cannon, W. B.: *Bodily Changes in Pain, Hunger, Fear and Rage* (2nd ed.), D. Appleton Co., 1915.
5. Dunbar, H. F.: *Emotions and Bodily Changes*, Columbia University Press, 1935.
6. Reymert, M. L., ed.: *Feelings and Emotions*, McGraw-Hill, 1950.
7. Alexander, F.; French, T. M.: *Studies in Psychosomatic Medicine*, Ronald Press Co., 1948.
8. Seguin, C. Albert: *Introduction to Psychosomatic Medicine*, International Universities Press, Inc., 1950.
9. Wahl, Charles William, with thirteen authors, *New Dimensions in Psychosomatic Medicine*, Little, Brown & Co., 1964.

TWO ❧ *Be Good to Yourself*

he above title is oftentimes the parting message of friend to friend — "Be good to yourself." And in most instances both the speaker and the listener are unaware that this philosophy is a basic principle of true psychology and true religion. But it definitely is; therefore if we would reach the contented and cheerful life, we must be good to ourselves.

Several years ago a farmer passed from this world leaving his widow and five little children. One world had ended for them, but she opened up a new one with the view that they had God above them, the soil beneath them and each other at their side; and thus with this combination she concluded that they would make it. The years passed and they more than made it. Each child made such a mark in the world that it attracted wide attention. As interest grew in this intriguing story of success, mothered and nurtured in the hills, a magazine sent a reporter to interview the gracious and God-fearing, humble and hard-working mother to learn the secret of her accomplishments, to ascertain how she with so little gave her children so much. She answered the question by saying, "Being I don't have much education, I just had to use my head." She had never had a course in psychology, but, in using her head, she taught them by word and deed the graceful and stalwart conditions of health and happiness, well-being and joy. She cultivated the following:

1) Love. She had love in her heart which she manifested

toward them. In turn they loved her and each other. She had no hate toward anybody nor harbored any bitterness because of the blow that had befallen her; and they, too, grew up free of animosity and resentment.

2) Cheerfulness. She was cheerful and happy in her tireless toil. They could see it because she sang much as she worked. And there was play too. Life was held in balance with the right proportion of each. There was an old organ which was often the focal point as they gathered to play and sing. But that house was filled with a sweeter melody that any organ music — the music of their hearts.

3) Work. She knew no rule for success would work unless they did. She put inspiration into her children and took perspiration out of them. They had to work to live. She had read in her Bible "that if any would not work, neither should he eat." She believed in work and so had her parents before her. Work came naturally just like breathing, and a willing mind lightened it. There was neither grumbling nor complaining nor self-pity. They did not feel that fate had slapped them with an unkind hand by demanding work. The day was a period of glad labor and the night a time of sweet rest. Rest is pleasant only to those who pay the price of work for it.

> *Each morning sees some task begun;*
> *Each evening sees it close;*
> *Something attempted, something done,*
> *Has earned a night's repose.*
> — THE VILLAGE BLACKSMITH, LONGFELLOW

4) Optimism. The optimism of her heart unaffectedly and softly gleamed in her face like warm welcome rays of light breaking across the hills of the east. As this farm widow broke

the soil and planted the seeds she saw nutritious bread — not wasted toil; and as clouds appeared she saw silver linings that would water her crops — not destructive storms. Sometimes she was wrong, but she was right enough times to more than justify the bright outlook on life. Every project was a work of hope. Each time she placed the eggs under a setting hen she entertained the fond expectation of a good hatch of little chicks; and she and her children would discuss this expectancy with excited anticipation. With hope standing as doorkeeper of their hearts, fear was not permitted to enter.

5) Religion. It might have been hard for this mother to eloquently define religion, but there is one thing sure — she knew how to eloquently demonstrate it. Her glory, however, consisted not in never stumbling, but in always rising every time she fell. Most of her time was not spent sitting in sackcloth and ashes, but in lighting fires in the hearts of her children. She instilled in them the idea that religion is not just a cloak to wear on Sundays, but an armor to wear every day; and it shielded them against the "slights and arrows" of opposing forces. The remarkable and victorious thing is — ironclad as they were — they hardly recognized the "slings and arrows" as such when they came. They were poor in money but right in faith — faith-rich in God and man. It was their shield against the darts of doubt and dismay.

She could have become her worst enemy, life-shortening and happiness-shattering, by crawling into a self-made prison of despondency and helplessness, gulping tranquilizer after tranquilizer which would have doctored the symptoms but not the cause. Instead, she befriended herself, prevented the cause, by helping, loving, accepting and adjusting herself.

If we would attain the good life of robustness and vigor, peace and contentment — if we would be free — we must begin with self and do the same things, as follows:

• *Help yourself.* The Creator expects a person to help himself. The lower creatures are largely finished by nature, but man is different — he must finish himself. This being true, then heredity counts the least in man of all the creatures, because conscious uplifting forces count the most. At birth his brain is least finished, his growing state longest, his capacity for improvement greatest and his proneness to social impressions keenest. All of this means that man is a creature of responsibility put at the helm of his own ship, to guide it as he sees fit, in life's still or stormy sea.

Wordsworth said it this way:

So build we up the being that we are.

I think it is distinctly clear that human happiness is the stake in this moulding and building up endeavor we call living. This is why so many people in every stratum of society are finding life grossly unenchanting. They were entrusted with life but have only partially formed it.

Their difficulties stem from something deeper and closer home than mere externals. As long as they stand in their own way, every pathway will be obstructed.

As long as a man stands in his own way
everything seems to be in his way.
— HENRY THOREAU

No matter what fate has dealt you, just step out of your way and it will be amazing how little the other obstacles will hold you back.

We must help ourselves by moulding our lives with the heroic and poetic philosophy:

So nigh is grandeur to my dust
So near is God to man,
When duty whispers low, "Thou must,"
I shall reply, "I can."

• *Love self.* While we seek to obey the command, "You shall love your neighbor as yourself" (Matthew 22:39), let us bear in mind that it is based on the idea that man should love himself. The trouble with some people is they despise themselves. Their frustration is a symptom caused by an allergy to themselves. They see too much in themselves they do not like.

A man can stand a lot as long as he can
stand himself.
— AXEL MUNTHE

The self-love presupposed in the above commandment is not indulgence in selfishness, conceit and glorification as one coddles and pampers himself. That is self-abasement, while self-appreciation is the right regard for one's character and ideals, emotions and powers.

A person will drive himself into neurosis if he perverts self-love into a futile pursuit in which, like a dog chasing his tail, he does little more than chase the tail of his own selfishness. The time will come in which it will be hard for him to distinguish whether he is doing the hunting or being hunted. While he is running after something, he will come to feel that something is pursuing and closing in on him. You are not going to find peace chasing yourself.

Excessive self-centeredness sees only self at the price of shutting out others, which is not true self-love; for love is kind and this is not kind, but the unkindest treatment one can perpetrate upon himself.

In *John Brown's Body*, by Stephen Vincent Benet, there is a vivid portrayal of a Southern beauty by the name of Lucy, who had so corrupted and misdirected love of self that she found it repugnant even to think of giving herself in marriage; for in reality she was already wed to herself. So standing before a mirror which enabled her to see her warped love, she addressed herself in this revealing vein:

> *"Honey, I love you," she whispered.*
> *"I love you, honey.*
> *Nobody loves you like I do, do they, sugar?*
> *Nobody knows but Lucy how sweet you are.*
> *You mustn't get married, honey. You mustn't leave me."*

That was a counterfeit love of self — not the real thing. She was actually suffocating in her own closed heart. Such a person can neither receive nor give love — the capacity is not there. What some have erroneously thought was a heart receptive to love was only a hunger for approval, approbation and exaltation. It is self-devotion which strangles all love that would go out and all love that would come in — neighborly, romantic and parental.

The happy life is found in loving yourself in its true meaning.

• *Accept yourself.* An acceptance of self is essential to the tranquil being. Yet so many have not accepted themselves and thereby torment themselves with inward tussles that could be avoided.

Jesus emphasized the absolute necessity of self-acceptance by asking this question: "Which of you by taking thought can add one cubit unto his stature?" Our height cannot be changed up or down by worrying about it.

Our encumbrances may be severe and even unyielding; but

in accepting ourselves as we are, we get on the road to happiness. One woman said, "The happiest day of my life was the day I decided I could never win a beauty contest."

I am especially fond of the homely but profound philosophy in *Green Pastures*, given by Noah who said, "I ain't very much, but I'se all I got."

We must accept the fact that different people have different abilities and diverse characteristics. The Bible teaches this in the Parable of the Talents (Matthew 25:14-30) and we see it in everyday life. It is a reality and we should face it. If we cannot do what we would, we can still find the good life by doing what we can. The little bird does not grumble because it cannot bark; for it can sing and it does so enrapturingly.

There is nothing to gain in fretting about what we do not have. If we would have peace, let us accept ourselves as we are, make peace with our limitations, and start from there a program of self-betterment. History shines with the names of those who did this.

Our problem is not to remake ourselves, but to do the best we can with what we have.

Fanny J. Crosby, one of the most famous song writers of all times, became blind when she was only six weeks old. She accepted herself and conquered the handicap. In later years she commented: "I am the happiest soul living. If I had not been deprived of my sight, I would never have received so good an education, nor have been able to do good to so many people." This was better than groping the streets of beggary and dismay.

Robert Louis Stevenson never saw a well day in his life; but he refused to bow to low spirits and left to the coming generations a rich legacy of literature.

Glenn Cunningham, a champion miler of his day, in early life was crippled in a schoolhouse fire. The professional opinion was that he would never walk again. But his dauntless courage proved them wrong. He went from following a plow, leaning on it as he walked, to tireless exercises and eventually to a place in athletic renown. He suffered a misfortune, recognized it, and then redeemed himself.

Sir Walter Scott was lame, but it did not deter him. He accepted it gracefully, and his biography reveals an enthusiastic, radiant, well-integrated being.

History's roster of the greats has paid little attention to personal handicaps.

Never — never — never accept the paralyzing doctrine of fatalism, reducing yourself to a robot!

Accept yourself! And be on your way!

• *Adjust yourself.* The fortunes of life are so changing that we are constantly called upon to adjust ourselves. And blessed is the person who can do it.

There is a tendency on the part of humanity to long for things to be otherwise than they are. "If only I could be placed in another setting, how much happier I would be!" "Oh, that I had…" These are the disheartening words of the malcontents. But a change of settings will only change the place, not the person; and where one is is not as important as what he is. Climbing from the valley to the mountain peak is not the solution to maladjustment.

There is a lesson for us in the fable of the beetle and the weather-cock. "How fine," said the beetle, "to be up there; what splendid views; how clear the atmosphere!" "Yes," said the weather-cock, "and if you were up here, you would know how hard the wind blows."

Some people make themselves miserable and worry themselves sick about their situation. Sometimes a situation cannot be changed for the better, but we can better ourselves by changing ourselves to fit it. For instance, if we are caught in a storm-cloud, there is no need to fuss about it; accept it and try to see the rainbow.

A philosopher who was passing through a store filled with articles of luxury and taste made himself content with this simple remark: "Lord, how many things are in the world, that Diogenes hath no need."

Some of the greatest success stories have their settings in the most trying situations. Some of the renowned works of literature were penned by men in prison: some of O. Henry's best stories, *Pilgrim's Progress* and others. These men had adjusted themselves.

There is a plant in Palestine known as the Rose of Jericho, which flourishes under the most diverse and adverse circumstances — in the hot desert, in the rocky crevices, by the dusty wayside, in the rubbish heap. Even more amazing, the fierce hot wind will sometimes tear it from its place and fling it far out to sea, and there, driven by the storm and tossed by the salt waves, it still lives and grows. How does it manage to do it? Acceptance. It accepts the circumstances under which it must live.

Happy people are like that.

Life is still what you make it.

So be good to yourself.

THREE   *Get Out of Yourself*

ears ago a man of deep insight, a country philosopher in our little village, said of a disgruntled and miserable man in the community: "Sam is rather tightly fenced in from every direction by Sam. If Sam ever finds peace and satisfaction, he is going to have to tear down the fences and break out of Sam."

Sam's ailment was "I" trouble. About all he could see was Sam. That is why he fenced himself in by Sam, but the plot was too small for him to be happy — just a prison for his own soul.

> *Oh, doom beyond the saddest guess,*
> *As the long years of God unroll,*
> *To make thy dreary selfishness*
> *The prison of a soul.*
> — JOHN GREENLEAF WHITTIER

The unhappiest person and the most self-centered person I know are one and the same person. An exaggerated consciousness of self habitually focuses the attention inwardly until outside interests have little appeal — the result is boredom.

• *The Master Teacher stated a long time ago that man lives his real self where his treasures are.* He put it this way: "For where your treasure is, there will your heart be also," (Matthew 6:21). No poised person lives merely where his body occupies space.

25

Years ago Robert Southwell said, "Not where I breathe, but where I love, I live." Of course, if his love had been self-love, then he would have lived where he breathed. But his love was elsewhere and that is where he lived. Our family may be scattered, but if we love them, that is where we live. We walk and talk with them, laugh with them and cry with them. What happens to them, happens to us. Our real self is extended to where our devotions or treasures are.

• *Nothing in this world but a person can live outside itself.* We can become so absorbed in an outside interest that we live in it rather than ourselves. Our love for another or a cause can become so great that we live within that person or that espousal rather than self. A mother said, "The happiest days of my life were when my children were little. They needed me to do things for them they could not do for themselves. I lived for my children."

• *Happiness comes from losing yourself.* Jesus nineteen hundred years ago laid down this principle for the abundant and enjoyable life: "He who finds his life will lose it; and he who loses his life for My sake will find it" (Matthew 10:39). Jesus ran His own lost and found column; and there is more to it than watches and diamonds, dogs and cats — man's happiness is there. Some have lost it. Others have found it. He that finds his life within himself shall lose it; but he that loses his life outside of himself shall find it.

The world's greatest book on psychology is the Bible. The greatest cause in which we can lose ourselves is God's service, for it includes all the principles which can take us out of our selfish selves and extend us to God and others.

We can find a new life of delightful satisfaction in losing ourselves. We must lose ourselves in a game to be thrilled by it. We must forget ourselves in music to enjoy its rapture. We have to put ourselves into our employment to find it pleasant and satisfying. We have to go out to our friends to enjoy their friendship.

As the little flower seed never becomes beautiful and fragrant until it breaks out of itself and grows up and blossoms, so it is with mankind.

If you would be well and happy, break out of that shell of self-centeredness, grow up and lend a helping hand to humanity.

Look up! and not down:
Out! and not in,
Forward! and not back;
And lend a hand.
— EDWARD EVERETT HALE

• *Helps in getting outside of self.*

A woman came to me with these words: "I'm not awfully miserable, but I'm not as happy as I should be. Can you help me?"

"Well, helping people is my stock in trade; let's see," was my immediate reply. Then I handed her a piece of paper and a pencil and said, "I want you to think of the unhappiest, most maladjusted person you know. Now, I want you to make a list of the traits that describe that person."

This is the list she made: "1. Thinks the world revolves around her. 2. What she does for others is for her sake and not theirs. 3. Self-conscious. 4. Touchy. 5. Spiteful. 6. Unforgiving. 7. Unfair. 8. Envious. 9. Shirks duties. 10. Gossipy. 11. Divisive. 12. Hateful. 13. Critical of others. 14. Wishes to be appreciated without doing that which commends appreciation and to be loved without loving."

As I looked over her list, I commented: "Not a very pretty

picture. No wonder she is miserable. Of course, this is an extreme case, the unhappiest person you know, but it does give us a lot of diagnostic facts. She is unhappy because of the person she is. So in order to achieve the beautiful life into which the most sunshine pours, develop and cultivate the opposite traits of that poor woman. Now let us make a list of the opposites, supporting each with a Scripture you can memorize and quote to give you strength in making that trait a part of yourself."

This is the list:

"1. Think of others. 'Let each of you look not only for his own interests, but also for the interests of others.' (Philippians 2:4).

"2. Help others for their good rather than for the praise of men. 'Take heed that you do not do your charitable deeds before men, to be seen by them. Otherwise you have no reward from your Father in heaven' (Matthew 6:1).

"3. Esteem others so much that you have a consciousness of them. 'But in lowliness of mind let each esteem others better than himself' (Philippians 2:3).

"4. Be long-suffering and forbearing. 'With all lowliness and gentleness, with long-suffering, bearing with one another in love' (Ephesians 4:2).

"5. Bless them who mistreat you. 'Bless those who curse you, do good to those who hate you, and pray for those who spitefully use you, and persecute you' (Matthew 5:44).

"6. Be forgiving. 'But if you do not forgive men their trespasses, neither will your Father forgive your trespasses' (Matthew 7:12).

"7. Be fair. 'Therefore whatever you want men to do to you, do also to them' (Matthew 7:12).

"8. Keep self free of envy. 'Love does not envy' (I Corinthians 13:4).

"9. Shoulder your duties. 'Whatever your hand finds to do, do it with your might' (Ecclesiastes 9:10).

"10. Refuse to spread gossip. 'You shall not go about as a talebearer among your people' (Leviticus 19:16).

"11. Be a peacemaker. 'Blessed are the peacemakers: for they shall be called the children of God' (Matthew 5:9).

"12. Love. If I 'have not love, it profits me nothing' (I Corinthians 13:3).

"13. Be tolerant of others. 'Judge not that ye be not judged' (Matthew 7:1).

"14. Expect love and appreciation from others only in keeping with what you sow or deserve. 'For whatsoever a man soweth, that shall he also reap' (Galatians 6:7)."

The Best Will Come Back to You

Give love, and love to your heart will flow,
  A strength in your utmost need;
Have faith, and a score of hearts will show
  Their faith in your word and deed.

For life is the mirror of king and slave,
  'Tis just what you are and do;
Then give to the world the best you have,
  And the best will come back to you.
                        — MADELINE BRIDGE

• *Some practical suggestions.*

As her eyes sparkled with appreciation she commented: "This is wonderful and I'm sure it will give me a new lease on life and a new experience of happiness — and I've had it all the time at home in my Bible. Do you have any other suggestions ?"

"Yes, here are a few simple ones; and as you do them, it will start your mind to working in the right direction and you can see and increase such activities.

"1. Think of others. Begin by putting up this little motto in your home: 'Others live here, too.' It can help the whole family.

"2. Do good unto others. Clean up the house for the sick woman down the street. Get joy out of cooking what your husband and children especially like. Attend weddings, funerals and showers and so express yourself as a blessing to others. Send greeting cards to your friends.

"3. Praise others. See good in them and let them know you feel that way.

> *It is in a certain degree to be a sharer*
> *in noble deeds to praise them with all our heart.*
> — LA ROCHEFOUCAULD

"4. Pray for others. Dear God, I know that Mary is having a hard time. Her burdens are heavy. He husband is sick. It takes a strong woman to stand up under her load. Give her strength proportionate to her needs. Help me to help her. Make me thoughtful to encourage her...

"5. Be hospitable. Invite others into your home. Have a party for them. Be different from the egocentric woman who had the tea party for herself.

A Tea Party

I had a little tea party
This afternoon at three.
'Twas very small —
Three guests in all —
Just I, Myself and Me.

30

Myself ate all the sandwiches,
While I drank up the tea;
'Twas also I who ate the pie
And passed the cake to Me.

"6. Laugh at self. This shows that you have grown out of the narrow confines of childhood and can see yourself from where others see you. It makes life more pleasant; for egocentrics cannot be laughed at — it is agony. Children enjoy laughter, but not if it is directed toward them. Deficient humor is an exhibition of immaturity."

• *We can all find health-invigorating happiness just outside the door of self.* The self-centered person tries to leap on happiness; but when he lands, it is not there. The reason is every leap is within himself. Spring outside yourself, and there just outside the door you will find happiness.

Who seeks within for happiness
  Will find it not.
It stands a guest unheeded at thy very door today.
Open thine eyes to see,
Thine ears to hear,
Thy heart to feel,
The call for touch of human sympathy;
In answering this there is
And close outside thee sits
The guest thou soughtest in vain within.
ADAPTED — CAROLINE S. WOODRUFF

31

FOUR  *Pull Yourself Together*

$\mathcal{O}$n two sides of my office the walls are made of antique bricks. When I first saw those old bricks they were a scattered, haphazard, useless mass which had been taken from the chimney of an old house and dumped at random on the ground. A useless accumulation of weakness and ugliness became a useful structure of strength and beauty. The difference is in singleness and unification. The possibilities were there all the time. All that was needed was to bring the loose pieces together and mortar them into a single structure. Ugliness was transformed into beauty and weakness grew into strength; and the thing that did it was the putting together the scattered fragments. In their scatteredness those bricks were nothing; but in their harmonious togetherness they are a strong wall.

Individuals are like that. One is like a helter-skelter pile of bricks; but another who has the same materials — like a wall is organized into a well integrated unified being.

• *Every person is constantly called upon to deal with the problems of a disorganized life.* We get rattled; we go to pieces — all because we get disorganized. By bringing the thoughts, desires and aims together, one achieves poise, peace, serenity. But if he permits the disorganized, internal state to multiply, then he becomes as many conflicting selves as there are conflicting whims and desires — a person of multiple selves in which each self struggles with all the others. The result is tensions. A discordant life with many forces pulling at each other can never be anything but miserable.

• *One of the necessary secrets of happiness is: Pull yourself together.* The chaotic and unfocused life knows no rest. The person who finds peace and happiness must bring himself together into a reasonably high degree of oneness.

The conflicting thoughts, wishes and purposes must be coordinated and integrated into a unified, effective personality. As this is accomplished, life is consequently lived with less tensions and more internal peace.

If we are unhappy, it is because we have internal conflicts which we do not resolve. We carry in our hearts the turmoil of many clashes. Happiness requires a person to face and handle his inner disturbances which otherwise would split him into several selves.

A few years ago a disturbed man who came to my office said, "I am going to have to get organized, for I feel like I am about to scatter into a thousand pieces. Life is fast becoming a nightmare. Can you help me?"

He knew what his problem was, but he did not know how to solve it. Some simple principles were laid down for him to follow and after talking with him on a few subsequent occasions, he became a new person with a different outlook on life. His latter comment was, "I didn't know life could be so good."

You ask, "What did you tell him?"

In summary, he was told: "John, no doctoring in the world will do you any lasting good unless it gets to the inside of you, for that is where your problem is; so we are going to have to recondition you internally. To do this, in the first place, you need a great center around which your torn-to-pieces-ness can be organized into a more harmonious being; and I am suggesting that center be God and then — blow, wind, blow — you will be prepared to face the storms outside of yourself. Secondly, we must change your thought processes and this can be done by associating with and talking to the right people, and by reading and meditating on the right thoughts."

As mentioned, he did this and found peace!

Now let us briefly elaborate on what we told him.

• *You cannot achieve internal unity without reconditioning yourself on the inside.* If you would prevent yourself from being pulled apart, you must renew the inward man. The Bible says, "Even though our outward man is perishing, yet the inward man is being renewed day by day" (II Corinthians 4:16).

The development and maintenance of a whole being is inward and spiritual, not outward and physical. The true psychological principle involved is expressed in this Scripture: "Man shall not live by bread alone, but by every word that proceeds from the mouth of God" (Matthew 4:4). A sustenance which nourishes the inward man is essential to peace and happiness.

Strength and riches are to be found within us.

> *There is nothing that makes men rich and strong*
> *but that which they carry inside them.*
> *Wealth is of the heart.*
> — JOHN MILTON

• *In achieving wholeness of personality, it is necessary that you live your life around a great center.* This will focus and consolidate thoughts and deeds which otherwise would be scattered, and in so doing prevent personality from breaking apart. Some achieve a small degree of integration out of such centers as a job, business, golf, fishing, hunting, and many other material aspects of life. To lose yourself in a person, occupation, cause, sport or game is wonderfully satisfying, because it is then that you forget yourself and all the fractional parts that are pulling you in opposite directions.

But a stronger center than anything that is human or material is needed to unite and integrate life's scattered and discordant urges into a strong, solidified personality. Our aims and determinations can never be grander or higher than the center that inspires them. This is why the greatest integration comes from having only God as the center in the innermost part of our being. It is there that our basic views of life and His spiritual resources for living are formed; and there is no center to form them like God, His unifying principles for living today and His solidifying hope for tomorrow.

Many distraught people have asked, "Don't you think a change of environment would pull me together?" It can be helpful, but no environmental change alone can integrate the loose ends of personality. A change of circumstances may encourage the unification of some distracting thoughts; but the happy coordinated self can never be achieved apart from a great center around which whole purposes and worthy resolutions can be formed.

The Psalmist said, "I will lift up my eyes to the hills, from whence cometh my help" (Psalm 121:1). God can help.

"I will lift up my eyes" from the low, earthly, personality-destroying distractions of hate, envy, jealousy, resentment, greed, covetousness, vengeance, inferiority, selfishness, unfairness and defeat to Him who can help me overcome them. By looking up, I can see my way out.

Isaiah said, "Thou wilt keep him in perfect peace, whose

mind is stayed on Thee; because he trusteth in Thee" (Isaiah 26:3). We must stop our negative thinking. Keep our thoughts off our troubles and discordant notes of life. Do positive thinking. Keep our thoughts on God and the strengthening and consolidating things which emanate from Him, like love, forgiveness, unselfishness, helpfulness, kindness, industry, meekness, honesty, purity, victory and things of good report. Do everything we can for ourselves and trust God for the rest without fretting, and the discordant notes of life will blend into a symphony — and that is music.

To live content with what you have;
To seek elegance rather than luxury, and refinement rather
*   than fashion;*
To be worthy, not reputable, and wealthy, not rich;
To listen to stars and birds, babes and sages with open heart;
To study hard;
To think quietly, act frankly, talk gently, await occasions,
*   hurry never;*
In a word to let the spiritual, unbidden and unconscious,
*   grow up through the common —*
This is my symphony.
— WILLIAM HENRY CHANNING

• *Associate with the people who calm and unite you.* Solomon said, "Make no friendship with an angry man; and with a furious man do not go; lest you learn his ways and set a snare for your soul" (Proverbs 22:24, 25). A little leaven leavens the whole lump.

Mary, in speaking of Jane, said: "I must break off my associations with her. She tears me up."

Jane's faultfinding, envy, gossip, gloom, defeat and hate

(though draped in pretended love), were making a nervous wreck of Mary.

We can be in the presence of some people and it seems they are a soothing balm for our troubled hearts. But others seem to turn loose a cyclone within us.

• *Spend some time every day reading great therapeutic thoughts from the Bible and secular books.* This will help to renew the mind by making us the sum and substance of our thoughts. Solomon said, "For as he thinks in his heart, so is he" (Proverbs 23:7). We will be united or divided, happy or miserable, victorious or defeated, depending upon what we think.

Here are a few of the many Scriptures with great strengthening and consolidating power:

My God shall supply all your need according to His
riches in glory by Christ Jesus.
— PHILIPPIANS 4:19

Surely goodness and mercy shall follow me
all the days of my life.
— PSALM 23:6

Cast your burden on the Lord, and He shall
sustain you.
— PSALM 55:22

FIVE   *Go One Way*

*G*et yourself going in one direction, if you would find peace and health.

One Sunday afternoon years ago a greatly distraught woman visited in our home. She had reached the place in life where she was an unhappy bundle of raw nerves. She said, "I am pulled to pieces. It is killing me. I haven't had a peaceful day in three years."

Then she told of a life of sin. She felt the urge to go back to her old life; but there was also the desire to go free, to find a higher and nobler life. She had a longing to travel opposite directions, to go both north and south at the same time. The conflict was tearing her to bits, to such extent that she had reached the point of desperation.

She went with us to church that night and I spoke on Directional Living. Toward the end of the sermon she wrote this note and handed it to my wife who was sitting beside her: "I've decided not to kill myself. On the way home I'm going to throw away this pistol in my purse." Well...that was the first either of us had heard of the pistol.

While not many reach the verge of self-destruction, all of us have the problem of moving in one direction.

• *Our peace of mind is dependent upon one-directional living.* The reason we cannot have peace of mind is because we have too many minds. We have one mind for one thing and another mind for something else. Those opposing minds have to be unified, as discussed in the previous chapter, *Pull*

38

Yourself Together. Happiness and health are achieved in traveling whole-heartedly in one direction without regrets.

A farmer, Henry Johnson, said, "I was once a dissatisfied discontented man whose health was breaking fast. I never found any peace until I got off that merry-go-round and started out in one direction."

All of us know at least a little from first hand about Henry's experience, because Henry's problem is society's problem — going in circles and getting nowhere. It is frustrating to meet yourself coming back.

• *All great men and women have had to wrestle with themselves to travel one way.* Ruth, one of the loveliest women in the Bible, had to make a decision for directional living; so it was a question of which way. This is never easy — the thing that harasses us is we want to go both ways.

After Ruth's husband had passed this life, her mother-in-law who was a widow and a believer in God decided to return to her native land of Judah. Ruth decided to go with her rather than return to her people and her gods — she was heathen. Naomi, the mother-in-law, tried to dissuade her but to no avail. In her insistence on going — one-directional living — she spoke and left for posterity some of the sweetest and most beautiful words to be found in any literature.

Entreat me not to leave thee, or to return
from following after thee; for whither thou goest,
I will go; and where thou lodgest, I will lodge:
thy people shall be my people, and thy God my God:
Where thou diest, will I die, and there will I be
buried; the Lord do so to me, and more also,
if aught but death part thee and me.
— RUTH 1:16, 17

We know that Ruth surely had clashing desires to travel opposite directions. On the one hand, there was the longing to return home; for what she loved most was gone, her husband. On the other hand, there was the desire to go with her husband's widowed mother; for there was a feeling of devotion and duty to her and by living up to it, she could find peace, happiness and satisfaction. We never find happiness by shirking what we conceive to be our duties. Ruth settled the problem by finding a fixed purpose; and by carrying it out, she found a new life of happiness and health, peace and usefulness. She became one of the most loved women of all ages, and a woman of such greatness that one of the books in the Bible was named after her. Centuries later her fame is known the world over. Wherever the Bible goes, the story of Ruth and her fixed course of life go.

The apostle Paul, as great as he was, also had to personally deal with the opposing pulls of life. He said:

> *I find then a law, that, when I would do good,*
> *evil is present with me.*
> — ROMANS 7:21

He, as all successful and happy persons are, got himself organized into a sufficient pattern of life to travel one direction. He could say, "This one thing I do" (Philippians 3:13). It did not bar him from troubles and perplexities, but it did give him the strength of a directional drive to meet his problems and that made for peace and satisfaction. He could say:

> *We are hard pressed on every side, yet not crushed; we are*
> *perplexed, but not in despair; persecuted, but not forsaken;*
> *struck down, but not destroyed.*
> — II CORINTHIANS 4:8, 9

Whatever it was that kept this man from distress, despair and destruction, is what all of us want, for every life has its own troubles.

* *To attain resolute living with a minimum of distractions, some trait, desire or purpose must become dominant over the others.* This resolves the problem of dissenting pulls or inviting crossroads. What we mean by this is there are various wares competing for our time, talent, loyalty and money. It may be the competitive struggles between morality and immorality, respect and disrespect, thrift and extravagance, industry and idleness, goodness and retaliation, self-approval and self-condemnation, assuring faith and wrecking doubt. Though many things are moral and legitimate, they cannot be had together. In that case, pick the thing you want the most and forget the others.

In harmonizing our conflicts a scale of values is involved. We must decide the kind of person we want to be and what we want in life and then get going on the road that leads there — that is how simple it is. This is why the Bible says, "But seek first the kingdom of God, and His righteousness" (Matthew 6:33). Something needs to be first. Seeking first God and His kingdom and His righteousness and all that this involves provides a predominant pattern for life which saves us from all frustrations and tensions of crisscross, haphazard and reverse travels. Happiness comes from making something so outstanding and dominant in our lives that we sacrificially and conscientiously give ourselves to it without regrets.

Many persons have a wrong idea about what constitutes true happiness. It is not attained through self-gratifications, but through fidelity to a worthy purpose.
— HELEN KELLER

But this necessitates the ability and courage to say *no* as well as *yes*. The happy life is the result of positive thinking, but we cannot think and act positively without saying no to that which interferes with it. Much of our unhappiness today revolves around our inability to pronounce the little word no. Strong emotions based on selfishness, greed, lust, irreverence and vengeance gain the mastery over the nobler self and create a case of frustrations and nerves. If we would attain the beautiful and tranquil life of health and happiness, learn when to say yes and no.

• *One-directional living does not mean there are never any cross-purposes or retreats.* Going one way is not an iron process that never bends or breaks. Some have thought this and because they experienced a deviation or setback in life, they became discouraged and gave themselves to more contradictory living which in turn produced more defeat and unhappiness. It can become a vicious circle in which one agitates and chases the other. We can better handle the problem, if we understand that the best and strongest characters have experienced turns and setbacks in the journey of life. "To err is human"; or to be human is to err.

Take the great apostle Peter as an example. He thought he was on such a straight course that he would never deny his Lord. He was wrong. But he did not permit the turn to doom him to a life of retreat and defeat. He later died for his Lord.

The Trinity River runs through our city. It has its zigzags, bends, horseshoes and whirlpools, but its direction is mainly one way — southeasterly. That river occasionally contradicts itself by flowing backwards; but, all in all, it knows which way it is going and flows in that direction.

One-directional living is like that. We may suffer a temporary setback, but with a predominant purpose in mind we get hold of ourselves and get back on course. This brings tranquility like the gentle flow of the waters.

• *Purposeful and one-directional living brings peace, because it puts meaning into each day of life.* It is then that every day has its meaning, and every day helps to fulfill that purpose. A man is satisfied, relieved and made happy when each day he puts his heart into worthy work and does his best; but what he says or does otherwise gives him no peace.

> *Look to this day, for it is life. In its brief course*
> *lie all the verities and realities of your existence;*
> *the bliss of growth, the glory of action, the splendor*
> *of beauty. For yesterday is but a dream, and tomorrow*
> *is only a vision; but today, well lived, makes every*
> *yesterday a dream of happiness and every tomorrow*
> *a vision of hope. Look well, therefore, to this day;*
> *such is the salutation of the dawn.*
> — FROM THE SANSKRIT

 *Think With Wings*

hink positively. Think progressively. Think constructively. Put wings on your thoughts!

• *The measure of a person is in his or her thoughts.* "For as he thinks in his heart, so is he" (Proverbs 23:7). This was Solomon's total of a man, his strength or weakness, his courage of cowardice, his peace or confusion and his happiness or gloom. He is what he thinks.

> *A man's life is what his thoughts make it.*
> — MARCUS AURELIUS

Our thinking affects our health. Our emotional and physical health are very closely related to our thoughts. So good thoughts are better than good medicine. The preventive is always better than the curative; however, healthful thoughts are both. Our thinking can prevent troubles; or if they have developed, our thinking can go far to correct them.

Most persons, however, are negative thinkers and consequently produce in their lives the crippling and defeating fruits of negation, such as weakness, dread, depreciation, depression and failure. On the other hand, there are others who through the energy and explosiveness of positive thinking make their lives engrossing and invigorating, happy and healthy.

Williams James, one of the world's most recognized psychologists, said there is dynamic power in thinking:

*The greatest discovery of my generation is that
human beings can alter their lives by altering
their attitudes of mind.*

The Bible, of course, had been teaching this principle for centuries, as seen in Solomon's quotation which was given at the outset of the chapter.

William James further stated:

*Believe that life is worth living, and your belief
will create the fact.*

There is power in believing. What you believe, in keeping with reality, has a way of happening. Anybody who starts thinking he is strong, will find strength; that he can bear what is placed upon him, will hold up; that he can overcome, will triumph.

But the opposite is just as true. Think negatively and our lives will be shrouded with gloom and despair. One negative sickly man said, "I always expect the worst and I have never been disappointed yet."

But a vibrant man with a healthy outlook said, "I always expect the best and have never been disappointed; though I do not always obtain it to the fullest, I always receive at least a measure and am greatly blessed in the expectation."

The difference was in their thinking.

Thinking makes us what we are. Negative thinking is self-destructive. Positive thinking is self-creative. Think happiness and we will be happy. Think misery and we will be miserable.

One pessimistic thinker said, "When I feel good, I always feel bad; because I know I am going to feel worse later."

But the optimistic thinker says, "When I feel bad, I always feel good; because I know I am going to feel better later."

Happiness it seems, has no logic. It is not to be found in

the facts of our lives, but rather in the thoughts we entertain relative to those facts.

• *Learn to say, "I can" and a new world of sunshine will beam upon you.* The apostle Paul mastered this art of positive thinking. He said, "I can do all things through Christ who strengthens me" (Philippians 4:13). He knew no burden would be placed on him he could not bear and no difficulty would arise he could not handle — that is, with the Lord's help. Positive thinking gave him the unconquerable spirit and the heroic life. It was his philosophy that no one is beaten unless his thoughts are beaten, that this is where we win or lose. Thus he could say, "We are hard pressed on every side, yet not crushed; we are perplexed, but not in despair; persecuted, but not forsaken; struck down, but not destroyed" (II Corinthians 4:8, 9).

"I can" discounts present and future difficulties. Worry is the art of appropriating today's and tomorrow's troubles to present misery; but happiness is the accomplishment of discounting today's and tomorrow's troubles to present joy. "I can" is not a mere fanciful statement, but the most practical principle in creating a happy and worthwhile life. It will work. It worked for Paul. It enabled him to find happiness not in his circumstances but in his attitude.

A war prisoner who had been confined for several days to solitary imprisonment stated that he made his own sunshine. He said that he knew the dangers of being locked in total darkness for a long time, that it could drive him out of his mind. So he devised his own plan for making sunlight. He manufactured it in his own mind. He spent several minutes every day remembering the sunlight he had enjoyed in past years. Though it did not tan his body, it did warm his soul and bless him. In a dungeon, he found sunshine in his thoughts.

• *Optimistic and unshaken thinking has the power to open*

new worlds to us: a world of opportunity, a world of usefulness, a world of health, a world of happiness and many others. The entrance to them has always been through the avenue of positive thinking.

Columbus, under the power of positive thinking, sailed westward in search of a new world. His companions, victims of negative thinking, wanted to turn back; but this man of history, this man with a strong will forged into iron by positiveness, prevailed over their fears and, lo, a new world appeared on the horizon for man to occupy.

The worlds which make life worth living can be occupied only through optimistic resolute thinking. If we are dissatisfied with the little world our thoughts have created and pulled in around us, then change our thinking and a new one will open up.

• *Positive thinking will keep you from grumbling, which is a form of emotional sickness.* All grumblers are disciples of negation. The complainer has his mental gears crossed. Before he can go forward, he just automatically shifts into reverse. His negative thinking is a habit which destroys zestful living. He has not learned that in order to have the hen's egg he must be willing to bear the hen's cackle. He sees the bad which is sickening instead of the good which is invigorating. A window, to him, is not something to let light in, but rather something to get dirty.

How much more rewarding life would be if he could view it with the attitude of Alphonse Karr, who said:

> *Some people are always grumbling*
> *because roses have thorns.*
> *I am thankful that thorns have roses.*

• *Thinking with wings will lift us out of range of the slings and arrows of little offenses.* It will protect us against countless wounds inflicted by a thoughtless, impolite and even cruel society. It will give us a character too big to carry a chip on our shoulder. What negative thinkers suffer in offenses, winged thinkers are spared. Those who are quickly irritated by little nettles will find their days miserable and their health broken. Bigness of thought is the best remedy for it.

> *Little minds are too much hurt by little things;*
> *great minds are quite conscious of them,*
> *and despise them.*
> — LA ROCHEFOUCAULD

• *You ask: "But how do we change our mental and emotional condition of despondency into an assured healthy-minded state?* How do we learn to think positively? How do we put wings on our thoughts?" Like all of life's greatest endeavors, it cannot be accomplished in an instant. The cure is not so much in observing easy rules as in following basic principles which remove the underlying causes of unhealthy thinking, as seen in the following:

1) Examine yourself in all honesty. Take a good look at yourself. Has negation destroyed your confidence? Are you afraid to think positively? Has it caused you to die a thousand deaths?

> *Cowards die many times before their deaths:*
> *The valiant never taste of death but once.*
> — SHAKESPEARE

Ask yourself: "Am I the person I wish to be? I was born a pleasant happy baby — what have I grown into?"

48

If the picture you see of yourself is that of a frustrated, balky, dissatisfied personality, do not blame others. That within itself would be the negative attitude. Start in to correct it by blaming yourself. Do not try to justify your attitude with the alibi: "I could think with wings, if it were not for…" — remember everybody has the problem of circumstances.

2) Desire the best even though it is challenging. A strong desire will mould your thinking. A husband was asked, "How is your wife?" He replied, "Oh, she's been enjoying ill health for a long time." Her being sick was more enjoyable than living up to duties. Some people do not desire to be positive thinkers, for it reminds them of responsibilities. It is easier to be negative. They get certain perverted satisfaction out of expecting the worst and waiting for it to happen. Some call it the piety of submission; others, the patience of suffering; and some others, the approach of practicality. But it is none of these. It is rather the sacrifice of better days upon the altar of easygoingness.

3) The assurance that we have the Lord's help will give us the determined will. A new outlook comes from the realization that the Lord is on our side. This banishes fear and gives us the courage to get on with our work. Our weakness joined with God's power is strong enough to conquer. While many profess to believe, they live in a state of practical unbelief. They forget that God exists. They forget that He cares. They forget that He aids.

We can overcome our paralyzing negation by filling our minds with positive Scriptures and by quoting them freely:

*My God shall supply all your need
according to His riches in glory by Christ Jesus.*
— PHILIPPIANS 4:19

God is our refuge and strength,
a very present help in trouble.
— PSALM 46:1

The Lord shall preserve your going out
and your coming in from this time forth,
and even for evermore.
— PSALM 121:8

4) Create a mental image of yourself as a capable and cheerful, likeable and vigorous person. Mental images have a tendency to develop into actual images. Healthy thinking will produce healthy feelings. See yourself as a ray of sunshine — not a gathering storm. It is the fog within that stops us rather than the storm without. Clear your mind with positive thinking.

5) Practice affirming good and pleasant forecasts. Tell yourself every morning: "This is going to be a wonderful day. God and I shall see to it. If solvable problems arise, I shall solve them; if not, I shall bear them and even then the unpleasant shall bless me."

As we approach new circumstances, we must develop the habit of saying, "This is going to be great." We may miss once in a while, but the record will sustain the optimistic view; and think how much more exuberant life will be.

6) Learn from the past — all wise people do. It will tell us that most storms we feared never struck; and that most lions we saw in the forests were only playful kittens; and that nearly every experience which hurt us at the time proved later to be a blessing in disguise.

I have seen the clouds break too many times not to know that this is true.

When I was a young minister in my twenties, I had a tonsil-lectomy. All went well for two or three days and then an infection developed deep down beneath the surface where the needles were stuck. It was before the days of penicillin. My condition became so critical that the perspiration, nature's way of throwing off the poison, was so great that one night the hospital attendants changed my pajamas thirteen times and the bed sheets five times. There was very little hope for me; but I never thought I would die. At the most needful hour, help came. My doctor attended a medical meeting in which the speaker from New York lectured on a new sulfa drug. My doctor asked him for some of this medicine, took it to the hospital, and began to give it to me. I immediately began to respond. I have always felt that God's hand was in it, that it was the answer to prayer.

Years later my father was seen by seventeen physicians, surgeons and diagnosticians. They said that he could not live more than seven or eight months or possibly a year. The aorta had become clogged. But again in life's darkest hour, a light broke through. We learned of some doctors in Houston who had just begun to take the aorta from a deceased person and transplant it in a living person. We took him there; the operation was performed; and he lived seven years.

I have seen marvelous things — too much to doubt.

7) Next, be thankful for what you have. Thank God every day for our blessings. Practice expressing our gratitude. "Be thankful" (Colossians 3:15).

Count your blessings and you will be surprised how well off you are — too well off to live in the shadows cast by negative clouds. Gratitude and affirmation just go together. As we become more thankful, we will become more committed to seeing the best.

SEVEN  *According to Your Faith*

$\mathscr{I}$t was an invigorating experience for me to listen to a man who came to my office as he talked of the positive power of his faith. He came not seeking the answers to life's problems but rather to discuss with me the answers he had already found through faith. His face beamed with confidence and joy. It was refreshing just to look at him.

He took a little Bible from his pocket and said, "I owe all my success, happiness and health to this book. I wouldn't have made the grade without it. I was a good clerk in a store, but I was tormented on the inside. I had ambitions to have a store of my own, but I was shackled with inferiority. I had restricted myself with self-created limitations of doubt. Ambition pulled me one way and misgivings pulled me another. It resulted in my becoming sick with tattered nerves. I had the right diagnosis of my case, but I did not have the right cure; and this only added to my tensions. In my desperation, I went through the Bible and underscored the verses I thought would help me the most in overcoming my problem of doubt and defeatism. Then I memorized certain ones. I said them every day. At first they seemed like empty words, but later they gradually began to take on meaning and to become an integral part of me. They changed my whole outlook on life and brought happiness to my troubled spirit."

These are the passages that gave him new dimensions for living:

According to your faith let it be to you.
— MATTHEW 9:29

*If you can believe, all things are possible
to him who believes.*
— MARK 9:23

*He did not waiver at the promise of God
through unbelief.*
— ROMANS 4:20

For we walk by faith, not by sight.
— II CORINTHIANS 5:7

He added, "I once did not believe enough to succeed and be happy. Now it is different."

Faith had transformed him into a positive, warm and victorious person.

What we believe or doubt has an important effect on health and happiness. No person can long maintain a well mind and sound body without some sort of faith. Doubt is a negative power which has brought defeat, gloom, restlessness and wretched health to the millions it has victimized. It is a physiologically accepted fact that when faith breaks down, the nervous system oftentimes does too.

Life does not seem worth living if it is only a listless and purposeless existence that consists of little more than the following of one day after another. On the other hand, our days can be a thrilling experience if they are lived in a faith which gives life a purpose and a destiny.

God gave each of us a mind which is his "thought factory"; there our thoughts are turned out. Whether our thoughts are positive or negative depends upon what we believe or disbelieve; and these thoughts determine our happiness or dismay.

53

This is how simple it is: Have doubt, fail and be unhappy; or believe, succeed and be happy. Believe in God, yourself and others, and results will start happening. Your belief becomes your thermostat which allows you to warm up or cool off, be optimistic and cheerful or pessimistic and sorrowful relative to the daily challenges of life. What we believe can change our whole personality and outlook on life. Faith gives life a zest. Oliver Wendell Holmes said:

> *It's faith in something*
> *and enthusiasm for something*
> *that makes life worth looking at.*

The world is filled with frustrated, insecure and fainting lives who will never find steadiness, peace and security apart from faith. If we are weighted down by negation and frustration, faith will give us wings to rise above our self-made woes.

No person's life can take on the harmony and happiness of one-directional living without faith in someone or something. No scattered life can be brought into focus in a maze of doubts and disbeliefs. As we believe, we pull ourselves together into an integrated being.

The disorganized personality is the victim of negative attitudes, created by doubts and fears. The cure for it is faith. Faith is the remedy for anxiety, self-pity, self-deprecation, inferiority, pessimism, apathy and fear. Faith will give us strength to "hitch your wagon to a star"; for it is a positive power that gives driving force.

• *We need faith in God.* As we believe in the Supreme Being, we become fortified and encouraged to handle the trials and vicissitudes of life. Thus it is understandable that as religious life decreases neurosis increases. Jung has said:

Side by side with the decline of religious life, the neuroses grow noticeably more frequent.

Life has its problems. Every heart knows its own threat of despair and needs the faith which wards it off. Every back knows its own burdens and needs the confidence which makes the load lighter. Every eye has a limited view and needs to behold Him who can see the road from the beginning to the end. We need this faith lest we faint.

The Psalmist was a man who had experienced some close calls in life. Looking back over the way he had come, he said, "I would have lost heart, unless I had believed that I would see the goodness of the Lord in the land of the living" (Psalm 27:13). His heartwarming statement describes the ups and downs of millions — they, too, would have fainted if it had not been for their faith. But on they went — fair weather and foul, good roads and bad — singing Paul's triumphant song of confidence:

I know whom I have believed and am persuaded that He is able to keep what I have committed to Him against that Day.
— II TIMOTHY 1:12

Feeling that their lives were in harmony with God's law, those victors experienced a heartening harmony within. Believe in God and conform to His laws — then it will be easier for you to think success, believe in success and be a success; to be adjusted and happy. Jesus laid down this philosophy of life in His great Sermon on the Mount. He said, "Seek first the kingdom of God, and His righteousness; and all these things shall be added to you" (Matthew 6:33).

A young lady who was a college student left the campus as soon as her class was dismissed and came to my office. As she walked in she uncontrollably broke down and cried. She tried to talk but could not for the tears. When she regained partial composure she sobbed out this story: "I have lost my faith, my faith in God, my faith in others, my faith in self. I don't know which way to turn." Her faith had been shattered and as a result she was several dangling loose ends. She needed to be pulled together and tied together as a unified being. Disbelief had torn her up; therefore faith could harmonize her. And it did. It took a few sessions, and she regained her faith, health and former outlook on life.

One of several things I discussed with her is this syllogism:

Something cannot come from nothing (admitted fact).
But something is (admitted fact).
Therefore, something always was.

Now what is that something that always was? that self-existent power? that first cause from which everything else has come? Cold, lifeless, dead matter? or God, the Eternal Spirit? God can be accepted as the self-existent First Cause, for when we say "God" all things are possible; but for matter — now that is different — to be self-existent it would have to be a god itself. So the Bible opens with the only reasonable explanation of creation: "In the beginning God created the heavens and the earth" (Genesis 1:1). We have never heard of a happy atheist. Their statements testify to their despair. For instance:

Voltaire, a brilliant literary man of France, said, "Strike out a few sages, and the crowd of human beings is nothing but a horrible assemblage of unfortunate criminals, and the globe contains nothing but corpses...I wish I had never been born." A dismal view of life!

Anatole France, another literary genius of France, admitted:

"If you could read in my soul, you would be terrified...There is not in all the universe a creature more unhappy than I. People think me happy. I have never been happy for one day, not a single hour." A sad state!

H.G. Wells, one of the most noted men of modern times, stated, "God, who was once the consolation of our brief life, and our refuge in bereavement and suffering, has apparently vanished from the scene." In his autobiography, he said: "I cannot adjust my life to secure any fruitful peace...Here I am at sixty-five still seeking for peace...that dignified peace...is just a hopeless dream." It could have been different.

Life has a way of teaching us that we need faith in Jehovah's watchful care. Years ago there was a grave illness in our family. After I had stayed up two days and nights without sleep, my father said, "Son, God doesn't need sleep, but you do. You can trust Him; so why don't you sleep some while He watches?" I did. Since then I have thought of those words many times. I was able to sleep because of positive faith. As life's passing years have called upon me to walk through the shadows, I have been able to find peace and rest because I knew the God in whom I believed would not fall asleep as He watched over me.

I have seen the value of possessing the faith to pray:

Give us this day our daily bread,
And forgive us our debts, as we forgive our debtors.
And lead us not into temptation, but deliver us from evil:
For Thine is the kingdom, and the power,
and the glory, for ever. Amen.
— MATTHEW 6:11-13

We need God's material blessings and forgiveness. It is

essential that we forgive others. Each needs to rid himself of all bitterness and hate. Ill will often causes ill health. Our keyed up nerves can be calmed in the belief that God can effect the principle that right will eventually win.

Let us have faith that right makes might,
and in that faith let us to the end dare to do
our duty as we understand it.
— ABRAHAM LINCOLN

With that conviction it becomes easy for us to live in the peace-giving philosophy that nothing good we do is ever wasted, that life's blossoms which may seem unfulfilled will someday, somewhere, bloom again.

Somewhere, for God is good,
Life's blossoms, unfulfilled,
Must spring from dust and gloom
To perfect bloom.
— IRA D. COOLBRITH

There is tremendous optimism in the belief that if today is dark, tomorrow will be brighter.

Beware of desperate steps. The darkest day,
Lived till tomorrow, will have passed away.
— COWPER

The night is long that never finds the day.
— SHAKESPEARE

Our nature and requirements are such that we can never have a feeling of security, peace and happiness without the faith so beautifully expressed in the immortal Twenty-third Psalm:

"The Lord is my shepherd" — Assurance which gives frail man strength and optimism.

"I shall not want" — My life shall be richly blessed.

"He makes me to lie down in green pastures" — He gives me rest.

"He leads me beside the still waters" — His leadership gives me peace and tranquility.

"He restores my soul" — He renews my internal strength.

"He leads me in the paths of righteousness for His name's sake" — God is God and for His own name's sake He will lead me in the good paths.

"Yea, though I walk through the valley of the shadow of death, I will fear no evil" — There is nothing to fear, not even death; for He is with me and will comfort me.

"You prepare a table before me in the presence of my enemies" — He is bigger than my enemies and will provide for me.

"Surely goodness and mercy shall follow me all the days of my life" — I shall not be forsaken of God's goodness and mercy.

"And I will dwell in the house of the Lord forever" — If this is not true, then all of God's work will end in failure without the accomplishment of one permanent thing; so it is too necessary not to be true.

It is this faith that keeps our hearts from being troubled. Jesus said, "Let not your heart be troubled, you believe in God, believe also in Me" (John 14:1).

• *Faith in people is another prerequisite of the good and pleasant life.* Our relationship with others is cemented and enriched by faith — our faith in them and their faith in us. It makes each a part of the others.

If we think the whole world is nothing but an assortment of depraved crooks, our natural reaction will be to withdraw.

As we withdraw from people, they will naturally withdraw from us. As you see, doubts about others bring on either separations from or conflicts with them. In either case, it tends to make life unpleasant. The best therapy for this difficulty is to believe in people and accept them. Most people are basically good — as good as we are — not perfect, but neither are we. If we mark off our list every person who is imperfect, we shall have no one left.

I have helped some people who later turned against me; but my faith in mankind is not shaken. There was one Judas out of twelve apostles, but Jesus never lost faith in and appreciation for the people. When we buy a bag of apples or potatoes we occasionally get a rotten one, but we still believe in apples and potatoes. It is better to get a rotten one occasionally than to do without them altogether. I had rather believe in all and be disappointed by a few than to believe in none. The law of averages has sustained my faith in the human family. Most people will come through, if they have half a chance.

• *We also need faith in ourselves.* Faith in self gives one the power to shape his life and destiny rather than be a piece of weak and helpless putty molded by what he calls fate.

> *Men at some time are masters of their fates,*
> *The fault, dear Brutus, is not in our stars,*
> *But in ourselves, that we are underlings.*
> — SHAKESPEARE

Faith switches on the power of human energy. It gives us the "I'm-positive-I-can" attitude. Paul said, "I can do all things through Christ who strengthens me" (Philippians 4:13). Faith reverses the defeat tendencies and shoots the person into forward motion. It generates the power of positive thinking. Faith means many wonderful, positive things: a shield against frustrations, fears and worries; a healing balm for sorrow; a stimulant for success, satisfaction and happiness.

When you believe that with the help of God and others you can, the how just naturally develops later. No matter how intelligent you may be, you are destined to failure and unhappiness unless you become confident. Confidence allows our minds to work for us rather than against us. In most cases our brains are big enough — the trouble is our faith is too small. We may lack initiative because first of all we lack faith.

Whatever our personal mountain is, faith will give us power either to remove it or climb it. It gives us internal strength to subdue, to obtain, to quench, to escape and to be valiant. The Bible, in speaking of some of the brave and heroic characters of the Old Testament, pays one of the most remarkable tributes to the power of faith:

Who through faith subdued kingdoms, worked righteousness, obtained promises, stopped the mouths of lions, quenched the violence of fire, escaped the edge of the sword, out of weakness were made strong, became valiant in battle, turned to flight the armies of the aliens.
— HEBREWS 11:33, 34

The sacredness of human life means no human being is ordinary; so we can climb higher than ordinary heights if we have faith. We can believe ourselves into greatness or we can believe ourselves into failure. If our nerves are edgy and snappish, it may be due to our belief that we are a failure while at the same time we possess an inner urge to succeed which refuses to be quieted. It has pulled us both ways. The cure is found in believing in ourselves. Failure in most cases is not due to circumstances but to the individual. When the mental view is colored with failure, then failure follows.

Self-trust is the first secret of success.
— EMERSON

Through faith each individual determines how much power to give himself.

If you think you are beaten you are;
If you think you dare not, you don't;
If you want to win but think you can't
It's almost a cinch you won't.

If you think you'll lose you're lost;
For out of the world we find
Success begins with a fellow's will;
It's all in the state of mind.

Life's battles don't always go
To the stronger and faster man,
But sooner or later the man who wins
Is the man who thinks he can.

Faith not only takes a person to heaven — it brings some heaven to him.

EIGHT  The Greatest
of These

Let me tell you about the two happiest persons I have ever known. For they have been great inspirations and joys to me. Several years ago they passed beyond the land of the living. Or did they? For much of them still remains. To live in hearts that appreciate you is not to die. One was a man. The other was a woman.

The man's house was called the House of Happiness. He was a wealthy farmer, a big landowner, a power in the church and a leader in the community. He was respected for his fairness and righteousness. His wisdom caused distressed and troubled people to seek him. His love made despairing people feel warm in his presence. He was popular. Occasionally someone who envied him would say hard things about him and start rumors about him, but it never rattled him. He had a large family consisting of a lovely, hard-working wife and eight children. At different intervals during the years he took into his home and reared nine orphans. When children in the area were orphaned everybody knew there was a place they could go — his home. He received no outside support in their upbringing. It was strictly a labor of love. There were children's diseases and many other problems all the time, but the remarkable thing is he got satisfaction and joy out of solving them. Ministering to their every care was the outlet of a powerful drive within him, controlled and guided by love.

The woman was a city dweller with modest means, but she

was a radiant glow of happiness. She had very little of what the world thinks is essential to happiness, but what they do not know is she had an abundance of the one quality most essential to happiness — love for God and mankind. While she was poor in this world's goods, she was rich in faith and love. She lived in a small apartment. She had no car. She had none of the fineries of life. She worked as a clerk in a department store to help make a living. Her domestic life was unpleasant, but she found happiness within a heart of love. That is where it is always found if ever found. This happy woman taught a Sunday School class of sixth-grade children. She gave herself completely to those children and they loved her. They would sit with her at church. They followed her and held her hands as she walked down the sidewalk. She took them home with her for dinner or to the parks every Sunday. They would sing, read the Bible and pray together, and together they would help the sick and other unfortunate people. She never had a bad child long, for he or she would soon melt under her spell of love. She called those children her Spirit Lifters, for she said that they lifted her spirit. But you and I know who lifted her spirit — she did by loving them. She lifted herself by lifting others. It always works that way. It did for her and it will for every one of us.

The man was rich and the woman was poor; so true life is not dependent on wealth, rank or station.

> It's not in titles nor in rank;
> It's not in wealth like Lon'on bank,
> To purchase peace and rest.

Then where is it obtained? In the big unselfish heart of love. Though their stations in life were different, there was one thing they had in common—love—and it was the beautiful and fragrant flower which grew in the heart of each and bloomed in the lives of others. Each gave self.

> *Not what we give, but what we share*
> *For the gift without the giver is bare;*
> *Who gives himself with his alms feeds three,*
> *Himself, his hungering neighbor, and ME.*
> — LOWELL

• *The Bible admonishes us to live on the high and happy level of love:*

> *But concerning brotherly love you have no need*
> *that I should write to you, for you yourselves*
> *are taught of God to love one another.*
> — I THESSALONIANS 4:9

> *Be kindly affectionate to one another.*
> — ROMANS 12:10

As we develop and manifest the qualities of love — patience, kindness, generosity, humility, courtesy, unselfishness, good temper, forgiveness, guilelessness and sincerity — we find that our spirits are lifted to new heights of joy.

• *Love lifts our spirits.* The way we feel toward others has a decided effect upon the way we feel about life in general. You cannot relax mentally if you have a tempest of antipathy raging in your mind. When we are at "outs" with others we have a tendency to be restless, depressed and unhappy. And what is the cure? Another pill? No! A pill will afford some temporary relief but will not effect a cure. There must be something better than medicine and there is — love. Love lifts us to new heights of joy. Life is a series of enchantments when lived free

65

of the sordid and ugly traits of malice, envy, jealousy, unforgiveness and retaliation.

• *Love is the most revolutionary word.* Love changes the world for man by changing his attitude. There can never be a changed world for us unless we change our attitude. Change our feelings toward human beings. People deny themselves of peace because of inner conflicts. Peace will come if we change ourselves on the inside from conflict to harmony. Treat others like you wish to be treated. Your life will be happy and satisfying if you live it in the beautiful and refined realm of goodness, self-forgetfulness and concern for others. But fill your heart with animosity and your life will be ugly and miserable. Sweet water does not flow from a bitter spring.

• *Love has a unique way of returning itself.* This is given as one of the reasons for our loving God. "We love Him, because He first loved us" (I John 4:19). Both love and hate have a way of giving and receiving in kind. Hate others and they will hate you. Love others and they will love you — that is, if they are untwisted, rational people. So it is a law of life: he who would be loved must love.

• *Love is a thermal power.* It is a quality of warmth. It warms the heart and gives life new meaning. If there is a coldness in our hearts which makes our lives frosty or indifferent, we must replace it with love. Love is the glowing flame within the heart which beams upon others, warms them and casts a delightful radiance that invigorates our whole society.

• *Love will give us a magnetic attraction.* Love is the force which draws God to man, man to God, and man to man. It is the pull that holds our world together.

The most powerful therapeutic agent in the world is love. Jesus laid down one of the greatest psychological principles in achieving peace and health in his admonition to love: "Love your enemies, bless those who curse you, do good to those who hate you, and pray for those who spitefully use you, and persecute you" (Matthew 5:44).

Two farmers became bitter enemies because of a fence which separated their farms. That fence was made of wood and wire and could be pulled down easily. But there was another fence erected between them much harder to remove than one of wood and metal — the barrier of hate. At first it harassed their peace of mind. Then it upset their production. Next it sickened their bodies.

Finally one of them called on his minister and spoke of the fence and his neighbor. After a while the preacher said, "You don't like him..." "Like him!" he stormed out, "he's a stinkin' skunk with no principles." The minister proceeded: "George, that fence out there on the farm is really not very important, but that one in your heart is. Unless you overcome this animosity it is going to destroy your living, your health and your soul. The thing for you to do is to pray for your neighbor every night. Ask God to bless him and his farm. Ask God to help you get hate out of your heart." Naturally he objected. But after much reasoning he agreed that he would try. That night he prayed: "Dear God, I promised the preacher I would pray for that dirty excuse for a man. You know how I feel about it, that I have mixed feelings, that I want him to be blessed and I don't want him to be blessed; but if you think it best, bless him as well as me." The next night it was easier; and the next, still easier. In time they became the best of friends, built a new partnership fence between their farms, increased the harvests on their farms and regained their health. When they tore down that fence which ran through their hearts, a new life opened up for them.

• *Our native urges can be angels of mercy or devils of*

destruction, depending upon their control by love or hate. Our native emotional drives like pugnacity, sensitiveness, acquisitiveness, curiosity, gregariousness and assertiveness are virtues provided they are controlled by love. But ill will transforms them into vices. We cannot neglect, suppress or expel these basic, emotional elements of nature. We are going to do something with them, good or bad, so let us give them outlet through love.

Combativeness is one of the emotional drives nature has provided us. It equips us for struggle. If it were eliminated, we would be ruined. The pugnacious spirit is essential to victory. The person with no fight in him is powerless. Thank God for pugnacity! That is, if it is controlled by love. But pugnacity guided by hate changes us into a nervous, restless erupting volcano of anger, unfairness, envy, retaliation and quarrelsomeness. Combativeness is not to be despised, for it is essential; but be sure love guides it.

Sensitiveness is another endowment of nature. Sensitiveness enables us to recognize excellency. It is a virtue to see merit, but the twisted and perverted form of it is envy. Sensitiveness well used makes happiness possible, but misused it tortures the heart. The hypersensitive person carries a chip on the shoulder and is quick to take offense. Sensitiveness is a good trait; so if there is a problem relative to it, the solution is not in emotional suppression but in emotional redirection.

Normal people are curious. It is first seen in infancy and later manifested through all adulthood. If properly controlled, it leads to achievement; if not, it spurs one to dig up evil and spread gossip. If affection is in the heart, curiosity drives you to greater joy and usefulness.

When good will is the controlling factor, all our impulses are put to doing good and this is happiness.

*Doing good is the only certainly happy action
of a man's life.*
— SIR PHILIP SIDNEY

• *But how can love be multiplied within us?* Both love and
hate are living things and living things can grow and multiply
or famish and die. Human beings are not born with rancor;
they acquire it. Love dies on what hate thrives. Watch yourself.
Love feeds on itself and so does hate. Cultivate the characteristics of love and love will grow. Here are twelve attributes of love,
as given in the Bible (I Corinthians 13:4-8):

Patient — "Love suffers long." Is passive, calm, understanding and will wait for the summons.

Kind — "And is kind." Is active, energetic and helpful
because it has a heart.

Unenviable — "Love does not envy." Has the feeling of bigness when others have it good.

Humble — "Love does not parade itself, is not puffed up."
Is not proud and swaggering; boasts not, struts not.

Mannerly — "Does not behave rudely." Makes you a lady
or a gentleman — prepares you to mix with all classes of society for love is polite and courteous.

Unselfish — "Does not seek its own." Thinks of others;
finds it "more blessed to give than to receive."

Slow-Tempered —"Is not provoked." Has composure, slow
to ruffle; can be angered, but not quickly; a pleasure to deal
with for it is not touchy.

Guileless — "Thinks no evil." Does not hurt people; never
makes capital of others' faults; places the best construction on
things.

Sincere — "Does not rejoice in iniquity, but rejoices in the
truth." Rejoices not in comparing self with inferior persons

and false standards; rejoices in comparing self with truth. Buys the truth and sells it not.

Forbearing — "Bears all things, believes all things." Conceals and hides; knows the art of silence as to others' faults which, without it, would annoy and vex; believes the best and searches for good.

Hopeful — "Hopes all things, endures all things." Desires and expects difficulties to be cleared up that the conduct of others may be made to appear proper and pure; does not give up on people; puts up with people.

Abiding — "Love never fails." Is adaptable to all circumstances and to all worlds in which we may be placed and still continues. Love identifies itself with another — another's accomplishments and failures, joys and sorrows — as seen in the above-stated analysis. When love is strong enough like in a romantic or parental relationship, the emotion is so powerful and unifying that it can best be described in the hyperbole of "one soul in two bodies." This was Mrs. Browning's description of it:

The Widest Land

Doom takes to part us, leaves thy heart in mine
Without pulses that beat double. What I do
And what I dream include thee, as the wine
Must taste of its own grapes. And when I sue
God for myself, He hears that name of thine,
And sees within my eyes, the tears of two.

• *Love is the best, the strongest and the most rewarding attribute we are capable of cultivating.* Man was made to love, for he was fashioned in the image of God who is love (I John

4:16). It is the silver cord that binds when everything else breaks; the outstretched hand that lifts us up when we fall; the soothing balm for the pain when fickle and thoughtless people press down upon our brow envy's crown of thorns; the instrument that pulls out the nails when enemies crucify us on a cross of hate; the golden stairway to ecstasy's heights which give a panorama of life like nothing else will; the rainbow in the eye which transforms life's every storm cloud into a gorgeous hue, and no matter which way the storm blows there is still beauty to behold and man's spirit is lifted.

The sweetest joy in life is found in loving and in being loved. We may suffer loss of health which weakens us, disease which pains us, sorrow which wounds us, disappointment which staggers us, business failure which bankrupts us, enmity which annoys us and betrayal which bleeds us; but as long as there is love, life is worth living.

Love is a story without an end, because "love never faileth."

And now abide faith, hope, love, these three; but
the greatest of these is love.
–I CORINTHIANS 13:13

NINE  Keep a Good Conscience

*O*ne of the most necessary conditions of happy living and sound health is an untroubled conscience. Happiness comes through the feeling of peace: peace with one's self, peace with one's record and peace with one's God.

"For our boasting is this: the testimony of our conscience," so declares the Bible (II Corinthians 1:12). The witness of a good conscience brings many joyful satisfactions into man's turbulent heart. It provides him peaceful earnests for today and pleasant anticipations for tomorrow. There is no rest like the peace in the house of one's own conscience.

> *There is no pillow so soft as a clear conscience.*
> — FRENCH PROVERB

• *There is something within our own making which can either tranquilize or disturb us.* It is a good or bad conscience. Conscience, even though it sometimes hurts, is very necessary; for without it man would be devoid of that faculty which brings his greatest joy — his own approbation. Without conscience, man would not be man.

If a person does what he thinks is right, that something within him called conscience approves and, in so doing, gives him a feeling of self-respect and peace. But if he knowingly does wrong, there is that internal witness which blames and tortures him. Man's doing right harmonizes and unifies him on the inside, but his doing wrong scatters and frustrates him. A guilty conscience lashes the soul as the waves do the shore, with all the unrest and turbulence of the splashing breakers. Thus conscience has the power to make us happy or unhappy, well or sick.

Daniel Webster said: "There is no evil we cannot face or flee from but the consequences of duty disregarded. A sense of obligation pursues us ever. It is omnipresent like the Deity. If we take to ourselves wings of the morning and dwell in the uttermost parts of the sea, duty performed or duty violated is still with us, for our happiness or our misery."

• *Conscience revives memory and brings up the ills of yesterday.* In a strange way it prods the processes of memory. It brings the past before us in perfect revelation. Conscience quickens the mind relative to unforgiven sins and stains and colors one's whole life. Authors, deeply impressed with this goading power of memory, have depicted it in the most descriptive terms. For instance, Walter Scott, in telling of a foul murder in a castle, stated that the blood so deeply stained the floor that, though the servants scrubbed and scrubbed, the dull red stains still oozed up through the oaken planks. This was his way of saying that man's evil deeds, unforgiven and uncleansed, continue to stain through the very fiber and substance of the soul.

• *The guilty conscience makes cowards and defeatists of all persons.* The smitten conscience fears and dreads without real cause. The person with a fearful conscience is so afraid that he sees his shadow as a stalking enemy to destroy him; every kitten as a lion to devour him; every bush as a tree from which he may hang; and every hill as an unclimbable mountain. He is like the man traveling in a wagon who said to a passerby,

73

"How much more of this hill is there?" "Hill, nothing! Man, your back wheels are off," was the reply.

• *A nagging painful conscience has such psychosomatic influences that it can drive a person into complete disintegration.* Shakespeare dramatized this fact in Lady Macbeth's illness. When the physician was asked about her illness, he replied:

> *No so sick, my Lord,*
> *As she is troubled with thick-coming fancies,*
> *That keep her from her rest.*

The physician was then asked:

> *Canst thou not minister to a mind diseas'd,*
> *Pluck from the memory of a rooted sorrow,*
> *Raze out the written troubles of the brain,*
> *And with some sweet oblivious antidote*
> *Cleanse the stuff'd bosom of that perilous stuff*
> *Which weighs upon the heart?*

It is a recognized scientific fact that conscience can make one sick. One cannot rest when his soul is disturbed with the horrors of guilt. There is no comfort for the one who lays his head on a pillow of thorns. An ill conscience can make a person ill in mind and body.

One of the many persons who have come to my office with a tormenting conscience was a religious lady in her late thirties. Her trouble was an overstimulated conscience. You say, "I didn't think anyone could be too conscientious." That is right, but a conscience can function beyond the purpose for which it was intended. Conscience is a voice which warns us before-

74

hand lest we commit a wrong or cries out and condemns us
later in our guilt. If we do wrong, it is the necessary duty of
conscience to censure and indict us, but when repentance has
been produced and God's forgiveness has been granted, it is
this assurance that should take the hurt from our conscience
and give us happier days. After conscience has worked on its
sufferer until a change has been wrought, then there is nothing to be gained by its continuing to torture its possessor. It
then ceases to be an asset and becomes a detriment. The
cloud of yesterday's sin, dispersed by God's grace but mentally
regathered by man and held over him by his reluctance to forgive himself, keeps his life in the shadows.

This lady stated that she was troubled grievously because
her prayer life was becoming more meaningless every day. But
her waning prayer life was not the cause of her worry; it was
rather a symptom. The cause reached down deeper. There was
a whisper within which bothered her. Another voice was with
her as Coleridge said:

> I looked to heaven, and tried to pray;
> But or ever a prayer had gusht,
> A wicked whisper came, and made
> My heart as dry as dust.
> —THE ANCIENT MARINER

The woman was a believer in God and had been a faithful
member of the church for years, but a sin committed in her
youth was haunting her. God had forgiven her years before and
she had become a woman of accomplishment, excellence and
trustworthiness. For years she had been happy in her church
life, but a mistake long since pardoned had for months
harassed her. Of course, it was maladjustment which needed

therapeutic approach — not censure but diagnosis. We should always make a distinction between cause and effect. Censuring the effect will not remove the cause.

I felt sure this reoccurrence of guilty feelings had its origin in a marital relationship that was not all to be desired, which she had refused to admit even to herself. She had chosen to dig up the past and place the blame there rather than face up to a present problem in her marriage.

After telling me that she had been taking treatments for three months and had made no improvement, she then asked me if I could help her.

My reply was: "You and I and God, all three of us, working together can help you. I want you to do two things:

"First, I want you to tell yourself that you are a good wife and that with God's help you will become a better one, that you are going to do everything within your power to make yourself a more pleasant, helpful, enjoyable, cooperative, efficient and satisfying wife. Remember: woman was created to be a helpmeet for man — you live up to it.

"In the second place, I want you to tell yourself: 'God has forgiven me and has blotted out every stain, and when God forgives sin He remembers it no more forever; therefore, I must put it behind me, too.' And I want you to read every morning and night the following Scriptures:

> 'Come now and let us reason together,'
> says the Lord, 'Though your sins are
> like scarlet, they shall be as white as snow;
> though they are red like crimson,
> they shall be as wool.'
> — ISAIAH 1:18

76

*For You, Lord, are good, and ready to forgive; and
abundant in mercy to all those who call upon You.*
— PSALM 86:5

*As far as the east is from the west, so far has He
removed our transgressions from us.*
— PSALM 103:12

*For I will be merciful to their unrighteousness,
and their sins and their lawless deeds I will
remember no more."*
— HEBREWS 8:12

Following the reading of those Scriptures, we prayed for
her to take God at His word. Then I continued: "Come back
next week and each week as long as the need exists for us to
talk out your problems. In the meantime, if you become too
depressed call me briefly over the telephone."

She called before the week passed for her appointment. I
knew she would, for her burden was heavy and she needed to
lay it on the heart of another for a little rest. After returning
for a few weeks and calling at various intervals, she regained
her composure, peace of mind and happiness. She found a
new life of joy in new assurances based upon the promises of
God. A clear conscience, cleansed and fortified by the assurance of God's forgiveness, was better than medicine.

The question arose in Act V of *Macbeth* as to who should
treat Lady Macbeth's ailment. A physician was called in on the
case. Listen to his opinion which is still the correct remedy for
conscience-hurting people:

*This disease is beyond my practice.
Foul whisperings are abroad!*

Unnatural deeds breed unnatural troubles;
Infected minds to their deaf pillows will
    discharge their secrets.
More needs she the Divine than the physician.
God, God forgive us all.

— SHAKESPEARE

• *If the hurting conscience is not cured, it may become the causative force in its possessor's becoming worse and hurting others.* Persons with guilty consciences may project themselves by accusing others of the mistakes they have committed. But what a miserable way to live! It twists their minds and drives them into a form of sickness. In condemning their own sins in others, these unfortunate people find only a mock and temporary relief from their discomforts. The liar enjoys denouncing lying in others; the swindler feels more upright by condemning swindling in his fellowman; and the gossiper feels cleaner by trying to find some fault in others.

Another woman whose past has its black marks has not purified her conscience, nor adjusted herself, nor become a blessing to the world — this she would deny. Her having erred is not being criticized — that would be inhuman; "for all have sinned, and come short of the glory of God" (Romans 3:23). But we are censuring her for allowing a hurting conscience to make her worse instead of better. While she has worn the mask of cheerfulness and good will, a storm has raged within her.

It could have been different. She could have been relieved of a suffering conscience and saved from the unholy life of a sin-searcher, gossiper and character-assassinator. When she hears of some defect in the life of another, in feigned innocence with the most joyous joy, she becomes all ears; and then

78

KEEP A GOOD CONSCIENCE

with the most delightful delight she becomes all tongue as she spreads it, not stopping to investigate whether it is true or false. Hurting others is of little consequence, for her great concern is to feel cleaner, bigger and more exalted. It has become pathological. Psychologists call this "projection." The person projects himself by seeing his faults in others, but in so doing he actually condemns himself. The Bible says:

For in whatever you judge another you condemn yourself;
for you who judge practice the same things.
— ROMANS 2:1

One's fault-finding is an index to his own personal problems. There is no surer way for a person to reveal his true self than his habitual condemnations of others.

• *A good conscience is so essential to the good life that the Bible includes it in the summation of God's commandment to man:* "Now the purpose of the commandment is love from a pure heart, from a good conscience, and from sincere faith" (I Timothy 1:5).

An uncondemning conscience is necessary to man's confidence toward God. "Beloved, if our heart does not condemn us, we have confidence toward God" (I John 3:21). This strengthens us for daily living. An approbative conscience is also a prerequisite to man's confidence toward himself. "Happy is he who does not condemn himself in what he approves" (Romans 14:22); and if he has, blessed is he that clears his conscience by obtaining God's forgiveness. What you think of yourself is worth more than what others think of you. The testimony of a good conscience is better than a hundred character witnesses. By achieving a restful conscience we can all have a God-given tranquilizer better than medicine.

TEN  *Seek Peace and Pursue It*

The enjoyment of good days is not an accident; it is an achievement. The pleasant life is always conditional and one of the conditions is the pursuit of peace. "He who would love life and see good days...let him seek peace and pursue it" (I Peter 3:10, 11). Peace and pleasantness just go together in a cause and effect relationship in which each promotes the other; and the result is the enhancement of health. So if we want health and happiness, seek peace and pursue it.

Peace is found where it is lost — in human attitudes and behavior. Thus we may find the good life of peace in the good-natured disposition that pursues the following ideals and principles:

• *Be forbearing.* The Bible teaches this beautiful and merciful disposition: "With all lowliness and gentleness, with long-suffering, bearing with one another in love" (Ephesians 4:2). Forbearance is an additive to peace within one's heart and thus within society. If you would achieve the tranquil life, be charitable. Remember that all temperaments are not the same, nor all the circumstances which surround people parallel. It is easy to say, "If I were So-and-So, I would do this or that." But if you were in that one's place, you might not know what to do — it is easy to talk.

It is to your advantage to make allowances for culture and circumstances, temper and training. Personal backgrounds are grounds for the more magnanimous spirit. Remember — many people have a self under surface that makes them better than we think; and under right influence those hidden qualities can be brought outside. This view keeps us from losing faith in humanity. It adorns our personalities with congeniality and loveliness.

As we become older, our appraisal of mankind tends to summarize as follows:

> *I see that good men are not so good as I once thought they were, and find that few men are as bad as their enemies imagine.*
> — RICHARD BAXTER

Apart from this view, we shall find ourselves erring in thinking too much of some and too little of others.

If we could only witness the terrible struggles passing in the heart of that one whose vivacity annoys us...if we could see the tears that are shed in secret, the vexation felt, we would indeed show pity. Love that person! Make allowances!

Forbearance is more than forgiveness. It puts the best construction upon everything, and, above all, never shows that some proceeding has wounded you. It speaks of one who has vexed you as follows: "She did not think, or she would have acted differently; she never meant to pain me; she perhaps was unable to do otherwise, and still suffers at the thought of displeasing me."

For a wounded heart, no remedy is so effective as forbearance.

• *In the pursuit of peace, go the second mile.* The Prince of Peace said, "And whoever compels you to go one mile, go with him two" (Matthew 5:41).

A good woman wrote: "In my own family I try to be as little

in the way as possible, satisfied with everything, and never to believe for a moment that anyone means to mistreat me. If people are friendly and kind to me, I enjoy it; if they neglect me, or leave me, I am always happy alone. It all tends to my one aim, forgetfulness of self. I think the one thing that interferes more with peaceful associations than anything else is selfishness. The Bible says, 'Let each of you look out not only for his own interests, but also for the interests of others' (Philippians 2:4)."

This woman had fought the bravest battle, which is within one's self; and had won the most valiant victory, which is over selfishness.

> *Real glory springs from the silent conquest of*
> *ourselves;*
> *And without this, the conqueror is naught but*
> *the first slave.*

Going the second mile requires meekness. The abundant and the delightful life of peace within ourselves, which is the first prerequisite of peace with others, is promised to the meek. The Psalmist said:

> *But the meek shall inherit the earth;*
> *and shall delight themselves in the*
> *abundance of peace.*
> — PSALM 37:11

A delightful way to live — peace with self and peace with others; and meekness which goes the second mile helps to attain it. Meekness is gentle, long-suffering and humble. It is not domineering, blustering or arrogant.

One of the greatest causes of strife is pride. The Bible says,

SEEK PEACE AND PURSUE IT

"He who is of a proud heart stirs up strife" (Proverbs 28:25). When we get to the origin of strife in a school, club, church, or business, the chances are we will find wounded pride. Someone feels bypassed, overlooked, unacknowledged or unappreciated. His egotism has been deflated.

> *He that is proud eats up himself.*
> — SHAKESPEARE

The distance from where you are to peace is more than a step — at least, a second mile. Whatever you have to do to trek the journey, do it; and you will be repaid a thousand fold.

• *Good will among associates is found in passing over another's transgression.* The Bible says:

> *The discretion of a man makes him*
> *slow to anger, and it is to his glory*
> *to overlook a transgression.*
> — PROVERBS 19:11

There is glory in passing over another's infraction. Let it rest! Ah! how many hearts on the brink of misgiving and disquietude have been made serene and happy by this simple suggestion.

Some proceeding has wounded you by its want of tact; let it rest; no one will think of it again.

A censorious or unjust sentence irritates you; let it rest; he who gave vent to it will be pleased to see it is forgotten.

A galling rumor has the splitting and tortuous force to estrange you from an old friend; let it rest, and thus preserve your charity and peace of mind. Ten chances to one, it is not true anyway.

A suspicious look is on the point of cooling your affection;

let it rest, and your own look of trust will restore that one's confidence.

Fancy! we who are so careful to remove the briars from our pathway lest they prick us, take such pleasure in collecting and piercing our hearts with the thorns we meet in our daily dealings with one another. Life is so much sweeter when we let the bitter experiences rest.

• *Be forgiving.* In the Lord's Prayer of example we are taught to pray:

> *And forgive us our debts,*
> *as we forgive our debtors.*
> — MATTHEW 6:12

How few there are who would dare address God each night in this manner: "Lord, deal with me as I have this day dealt with others; treat me as I treated those to whom I was harsh, and, from malice or a feeling of superiority, exposed their failings; others, to whom, from pride or dislike, I refused to speak — one I avoided, another I cannot like because she displeases me."

And yet let us remember: "But if you do not forgive men their trespasses, neither will your Father forgive your trespasses" (Matthew 6:15). He who cannot forgive obstructs the road over which he himself must travel.

There can be no peace with others unless we forgive; because, sooner or later, we will feel that we have been wronged. Then there is the trouble which stirs within us and later breaks out of us.

But the one who forgives ends the quarrel; then he finds calmness and concord, peace and pleasantness. Forgiveness is both a tranquilizer and a stimulant; a tranquilizer which settles nerves and a stimulant which invigorates health.

• *Peace with self and with others comes in gracefully handling the little annoyances.* Every day we are distressed by some one of those numberless little worries that inevitably meet us at every step.

The wound made in the heart may not be deep; but the constant pricks, each day renewed, embitter the character, destroy peace, create anxiety, and make our associations with others almost intolerable, which otherwise could be so sweet and peaceable. Life is full of those little potential miseries, if we allow them to so affect us. Each hour brings its own threat to our tranquility.

Here are some of the little disturbances: An impatient word escapes our lips in the presence of someone in whose estimation we would like to stand well. Then we worry.

A subordinate does his work badly, fidgets us by his slowness, irritates us by his thoughtlessness; and his awkward blunders disturb us, and our display of anger later disquiets us.

A giddy child in his clumsiness breaks something of value and more so to us because of its connection. Then we are exasperated.

We are charged with a message of importance, and our forgetfulness makes us appear discourteous and ungrateful. Then we suffer days of vexation.

Someone we live with constantly finds fault, and shows no regard for our feelings or preferences. It needles us.

But you say, "How do we bear life's little vexations?"

In the first place, we must *expect them.* Remember that no life is exempt from them. Every life knows its own troubles and every heart suffers its own ache. Make them the subject of our morning prayers, saying, "Here is my daily cross. Help me to accept it willingly. After all, these little troubles can help me to be stronger."

Secondly, *we must bend to receive our distresses.* If we wish to break the force of a blow, we naturally bend the body with the impact. The same principle works in receiving society's blows which beat down upon us — just bend with them.

Accustom yourself to stoop with sweet condescension to the simple wishes of those who surround you, if there is no compromise of truth or principle. Bending is the art of displaying an external sweetness that yields. It is not stubborn. The person who stands unyieldingly always feels the breaking blows because of his inflexibility. The live trees, flexible and giving, bend with the storm and survive; but the dead trees, firm and stiff, are broken to pieces. One endures the storm; the other is shattered — how true of us!

• *Be considerate.* When working with others, never laugh or make fun of their mistakes or awkwardness. If it is caused by stupidity, our laughter is uncharitable; if it is ignorance, our mockery, to say the least, is unjust.

Teach the unskillful with gentleness; show him the right way to do things; and many will beat a pathway to your door, seeking your friendship.

Be considerate of your friends; never annoy them. Here are four clear, precise rules, which will guard you against bothering your friends.

1) Always leave your friend something more to desire of you. If he asks you to go and see him three times, go but twice. He will look forward to your coming a third time; and when you go, he will receive you the more cordially.

2) Be useful to your friend as far as he permits you, and no further. An over-anxious affection becomes tiresome. Devotion

to a friend does not consist in doing everything for him, but simply that which is agreeable and serviceable to him.

We all love freedom and cling tenaciously to our little fancies. We do not like others to arrange what we have purposely left in disorder; we even resent their over-anxiety and care for us.

3) Be occupied with your own business — and little, very little — with the business of your friend. This infallibly leads to a favorable result. If he appeals to you for help, go through fire and water to serve him; if not, then whatever you do, just be sure that it is welcomed. In other words, "But let none of you suffer as a...busybody in other men's matters" (I Peter 4:15).

4) Leave your friend always at liberty to think and act for himself. Do not try to take over his life. Why compel him to think and act with you? After all, he might be right; if not, he still has the right to live his own life.

• *Be obliging.* It makes for goodness and peace to live in an atmosphere in which we make it our study to render others service and to ask the same of them. Our need of others is the link which holds humanity together.

Like begets like. We reap as we have sown. If we would get the best from others, see to it that others get the best from us.

These attitudes and patterns of behavior make for affable living with all of its attendant blessings — health of mind and body and a multiplicity of others. "Blessed are the peacemakers."

ELEVEN  *Cloud Breakers*

*A*despondent and despairing woman with melancholy spelled out all over her countenance came to my office with these words: "My sunshine has turned into clouds."

This happens to all of us sooner or later, because life is a mixture of sunshine and storms, encouragements and discouragements, joys and sorrows; and each has its accompanying effects upon the spirit of man. The effects we call moods; and these temperaments or mental veins influence all aspects of life — health and happiness, security and success. So in attaining the better and fuller life I need to keep the handsome and hopeful, valiant and victorious disposition.

When this was pointed out to the woman who found her world closing in with shadows, she asked: "But how can I maintain an all-will-end-well spirit in the face of clouds which show no sign of breaking?" How! ah! that is the urgent cry from a million voices on every shore in every clime. As life's storm-beaten pilgrims strain their eyes in search of a break in the clouds, it becomes the expressed concern of anxious hearts. How! how can I find sunshine in a cloudy world?

All of us have the problem of seeing through our clouds, lest we consign many precious days of our fleeting lives to growing tensions, gathering gloom and multiplying morbidity. We need a philosophy, a line of thought, that scatters our clouds. We need cloud breakers in the heart; then no matter how black and disconcerting life's weather may become, the hopeful light of fairer skies will break across our limited vision — and we shall take courage and press onward. As surely as clouds gather, clouds shall pass; and as the black night irrevocably settles, a new day dawns. The Bible says:

Then your light shall break forth
like the morning.
— ISAIAH 58:5

I have found in the Bible many cloud breakers, new day dawnings, which I have freely quoted to give me enthusiasm and vigor as I began to experience "let-down" feelings generated by gathering storm clouds on the darkening horizons. Here are some of those philosophical sacred principles with the recommendation that you memorize them; make them your compass and comfort; say them again and again in time of need:

• *Good Days* — "He who would love life and see good days, let him refrain his tongue from evil, and his lips from speaking guile...let him seek peace and pursue it" (I Peter 3:10, 11). Our days can be good or bad, depending upon what we put into them; for in the last analysis they are products of our own creation. We are not unmindful of outside forces which may be pleasant or unpleasant, helpful or hurtful; but as to whether they make our day good or bad still depends upon our own reactions to those experiences.

We are the pilot of our ship. It is not the wind, but the set of the sails that determines our direction in life's sea. It is the stuff we are made of rather than the fiery trials we encounter which fixes our softness or hardness; for the same fire that hardens the clay melts the tallow.

The society in which we live may be mistaken and militant, selfish and scurrilous in its opposition to us; but we can still have good days by clinging to a way of life which makes them. We can feel good by doing good, though others do us evil. This was true of the early Christians who, not counting their lives dear unto themselves, rejoiced in their persecutions. Their joy was not found in pain but in the gratification that comes from doing right. The story of their bravery and joy in the lion's mouth of trials and persecutions is more spectacular than any author's novel and more sublime than any poet's verse. Slander and suffering, persecution and privation were their lot; but there was a more excellent portion for them: good days, good days in spite of a world gone mad, good days which they made for themselves by doing good — ah! there was the difference.

If we do not like our days, thank God we can change them provided we are willing to change ourselves; for our days are made within us.

Good days are found in good speech which bespeaks a good heart; "for out of the abundance of the heart the mouth speaks" (Matthew 12:34). The happy life requires the bridling of a tongue that could run loose and the sealing of lips that could utter guile. Remember — your tongue cannot harm others without hurting yourself, for you are on the other end of it.

Favorable days are dependent also upon beneficial deeds. The pleasant life shuns ugliness and spreads pleasantries among others. We keep ourselves by keeping our brother. The world's shortest and sweetest biography tells of a life of concern and goodness for others — "who went about doing good" (Acts 10:38). That is the story of Christ.

Happiness, like a tide that flows in and out, will come back to you after you have sent it to others. So occupy that traditional house by the side of the road and be a friend to mankind. As they pass, give a cup of cold water to the thirsty and extend a helping hand to the downtrodden. Share the joys of those who smile and bear the sorrows of those who mourn. "Rejoice with those who rejoice and weep with those who weep" (Romans 12:15).

• *Heaven's Guarantee of Plenty* — "But seek first the kingdom of God, and His righteousness; and all these things shall be added unto you" (Matthew 6:33). This is heaven's infallible formula for obtaining the necessities of life — seek first God's kingdom and God's righteousness. This includes all the attributes associated with the nobler life: faith, hope and love, dependence and diligence, work and thrift. It excludes laziness and irresponsibility. God's way is not the way of the spendthrift or sluggard. "Go to the ant, you sluggard; consider her ways, and be wise," so speaks Solomon in the Bible (Proverbs 6:6). The plenteous life can never be found in either indolence or waste. The full cupboard is only for those who will do their part to fill it.

As we seek the higher life we will be raised by two sources: by our own seeking and by the hand above that lifts us up. The same two sources of power will supply our material needs: our work and God's help. This is an unbeatable combination. We must do our part and trust the God who clothes the fields and feeds the fowls. Jesus said in the Sermon on the Mount:

Look at the birds of the air, for they neither sow
nor reap nor gather into barns; yet your heavenly Father
feeds them. Are you not of more value than they?...
Consider the lilies of the field, how they grow: they neither toil
nor spin.... Now if God so clothes the grass of the field, which
today is, and tomorrow is thrown into the oven,
will He not much more clothe you, O you of little faith?
— MATTHEW 6:26-30

Putting spiritual things first gives us a tremendous driving power by eliminating all negative thoughts which burn up energy and waste time — doubt, faultfinding, hate, selfishness, vengeance and unforgiveness. The righteous life replaces these negative qualities with positive ones which strengthen, like faith, love, tolerance, unselfishness, magnanimity and forgiveness. It directs energies from the waste of negative thinking to the positive channels of construction and attainment. Thus this sheds light on why righteousness is good economics. Righteousness linked to the providential care of God constitutes an economic system so effectual and great that it includes the work of both man and God and reaches all the way from earth to heaven. You cannot beat that!

With God's help, as David expressed it in the *Twenty-third Psalm*, we can have a prepared table in green pastures beside still waters. And that is a fact! For "we are His people, and the sheep of His pasture."

• *God can overrule man's intended harm to your good* — "But as for you, you meant evil against me; but God meant it for good" (Genesis 50:20). These were the reassuring words spoken by the princely Joseph to his brutal and criminal brothers who years before had sold him into forced slavery. He had gone through the travail of servitude and the confinement of imprisonment; but, in looking back at those dreadful days, he saw them in their true meaning as only essential phases or hidden blessings in his life which was being shaped for rulership in Egypt.

We observe in Joseph's expressed thoughts that he had no rancor, no hate, no bitterness, no resentment, but rather possessed a spirit of forgiveness. His heart was too packed with bigness to leave any room for littleness. His forgiving, unrevengeful attitude of letting bygones be bygones had become a sweet-scented balm for his wounded heart. His magnanimity and gratitude were so abounding that they figured even in the naming of his sons:

Joseph called the name of the firstborn Manasseh: "For God has made me forget all my toil, and all my father's house." And the name of the second he called Ephraim: "For God has caused me to be fruitful in the land of my affliction."
— GENESIS 41:51, 52

In this story of Holy Writ we see the almighty hand of God overruling the plotted perpetration of evil by brothers against brother. The victim of man's hate became the object of God's blessing. Little men could not stay the hand of God. He gave them something to chew on that broke their teeth; so their bark was worse than their bite. Man makes plans; God changes them. Man tries; God succeeds. As much as the brothers wished to harm Joseph, they could not (though it appeared they had); because One bigger and smarter than they had His eye on him. They intended to harm him; they planned to harm him; they thought only harm would ever come to him. But God confounded the wicked and their intentional bane became their unintentional boon. It happens so often. So be brave; be patient. The last chapter has not been written yet.

Remember — right, like sweet cream, has a way of coming to the top; while wrong, like spilled milk, wastes itself in useless absorption. Remember — God governs and guides in the affairs of men.

God moves in a mysterious way His wonders to perform

He plants his footsteps on the sea
And rides upon the storm.
— COWPER

When the wicked throw out nets for the capture and containment of those they envy and hate, many men tempted to mope and women pressed to weep take heart from the words of the Psalmist:

They have prepared a net for my steps; my soul is
bowed down; they have dug a pit before me, into
the midst of it they themselves have fallen.
— PSALM 57:6

Because You have been my help, therefore
in the shadow of Your wings will I rejoice.
— PSALM 63:7

• *Returned bread upon the waters* — "Cast your bread upon the waters; for you will find it after many days" (Ecclesiastes 11:1). There is enough encouragement in this reassuring Scripture to give us a new lease on life. Yea! how we need it! for sometimes it seems the old lease has run out — so why try any longer? Disappointed and discouraged, dejected and downhearted, we are tempted to ask: "Why cast the bread into unlikely waters, foaming in their unfriendly restlessness, only to see it disappear behind the back of waves turned against us?"

When we are inclined to withhold the sowing, thinking that opposing circumstances will prevent the reaping for others and ourselves, this passage gives us hope and direction which are two of our most basic needs in life. Disperse the bread and later we will find it again. So let us hold to the principle that

94

good will come from good. There may be a temporary or even a prolonged disappointment, but kindness will eventually prosper its doer.

The cast bread may be carried by angry waves far beyond the caster's sight, but it will return. It may be driven by a turbulent and tempestuous sea into the darkness of a starless night, but a new day will dawn, bringing with it gentle returning waves upon which that bread will be afloat — and it will be yours.

The caster is even blessed by the throwing, for his arm is strengthened by the casting; and if there were no other returns, it would still be worth it.

We are thankful for life's reciprocal features which help us to see the bright side of life. As we stand at the water's edge and look out across life's unknown sea, it makes our days more livable to keep in mind that the tide goes out and the tide comes in and thus what we cast on the waters will return again. The world has a way of paying back in kind what we give it. Give consideration, courtesy, benevolence, kindness, forgiveness and such we will receive. "For with what judgment you judge, you will be judged" (Matthew 7:2).

• *Joy in the morning* — "Weeping may endure for a night, but joy comes in the morning" (Psalm 30:5). Life has its night and morning, weeping and rejoicing. We have no control over the day or the night. It is not within our power to prolong or shorten either. Our fussing and fuming will neither slow nor hasten the sun. But we do have the assurance that morning follows the night — so be patient.

Life has its tears — thank God for that which mellows the heart and keeps us in sympathy with humanity. Just as the day seems brighter after the night, so the sparkle of joy in the eye seems sweeter as it bursts through tears beginning to dry.

We have seen the tears which had the drip and stain of

fear or immaturity; for it was no time to cry, but a time to work, a time to contend, a time to test the metal. But we have also witnessed rivers of tears which flowed from the big hearts of courageous, heroic people. They wept because they were strong, strong in sympathy, strong in tenderness, strong in love, strong in the deepest of feelings. Let us not be deceived by thinking that a hard heart is synonymous with bravery. "Jesus wept" (John 11:35), and His courage has never been equalled. He wept because He was strong in the most admirable and precious traits.

Throughout the long night as sorrow flows from a wounded heart and as the mists blur my vision, I dry a tear now and then and strain my eyes in the anxious search of the break of dawn along a blessed horizon. And what bliss when the morning of joy breaks upon my tear-stained face. Thank God for tears. Thank God for happiness. But the joy would not be so sweet, if the tears had not been so bitter.

So during the long hours of the night, as my heart bleeds over a matter that seems to have no solution, be patient; yea, be patient for the morning of joy will come; I know it will come and then every tear will have its compensation.

Not the End

But a New Beginning

*May Your Joys Be a
Hundred Times a Hundred*